*Trust the journey ♡ Pattie*

# Round America

# with a Duck

## Pattie Baker

© 2024 by Pattie Baker

All rights reserved. This book or any portion thereof may not be reproduced or used in any manner whatsoever without the written permission of the author except for the use of brief quotations in a book review. Contact her at sustainablepattie@comcast.net.

ISBN 979-8-8757-4559-1

United States of America

The author believes the stories in this book to be factual based on her lived and learned experience. Others present may recall their parts in them with variations.

**OTHER BOOKS BY PATTIE BAKER**

*Traveling at the Speed of Bike*

*Food for My Daughters*

*Bucket List*

*To my beautiful country for letting me trust-fall across it, and to my hubby for trusting the journey with me*

# TABLE OF CONTENTS

Prologue —ix
*The number two question everyone asked*

**1**
New Kid on the Block —1
*Goat farm on repurposed tobacco land in North Carolina*

**2**
Rocky Steps and Groovy Bridges —32
*Throwbacks that feel new in Philly and New York*

**3**
No Horsing Around —68
*Horses and hurricanes on Route 66 in Missouri*

**4**
Heaven on Earth —91
*Alpacas and eco-spirituality in Kansas*

**5**
Time Makes You Bolder —122
*Backyard garden and bike joy in Colorado*

**6**
Altars and Halters —152
*Krishna Temple and llama ranch in Utah*

**7**
Hot Streak —181
*Winning gamble and melting shoes in Las Vegas*

**8**
La La Land —194
*Llamas and lavender in California*

**9**
Sweet Endings —216
*Beach to beignets from Los Angeles to New Orleans*

**10**
Making A Mark —241
*Permanent reminder to trust the journey*

Acknowledgments —244

# PROLOGUE

So 78-year-old Sister Jane from the Dominican Sisters of Peace was on the roof of the cabin checking to see if the composting toilet's vent was clogged. My little cabin stunk and no amount of sawdust would help. I was mortified, of course, but I *had* to alert her that there was undeniably a problem. I was departing this 80-acre/32-hectare alpaca farm and eco-spirituality center in Pawnee Rock, Kansas in two days and I couldn't leave things in this condition. It had been too good a visit the prior five weeks (labyrinth saga aside).

I had been sweating the, shall we call it, *bathroom situation* since the start of my 10,000-mile/16,100-kilometer journey across the USA via bike, buses, trains and working on organic farms two months ago. I know, I know, no one ever really wants to hear the actual details, but it was literally the number-two question (ever so ironically) I got asked when I told people about this five-month trip. For those of you queasy about this topic, I don't linger on it in this book, although it could, truth be told, be its own book.

Some of it had already happened by the time agile Sister Jane whisked up that ladder. Dragging all my stuff into restrooms at bus stations in the middle of the night. Tiny bathrooms on commuter trains, or none at all. The basic discomfort of using the toilet in someone else's home. But more was yet to come.

That choice seat, 14C, right next to the sloshing latrine on the bus through Death Valley in 115 degrees Fahrenheit/46 degrees Celsius. On rattling long-distance trains while slicing through the Rockies and while hugging the border in Mexico. Behind a tree in a crowded public park in Denver. Under a rain poncho on a curb in Kansas. With pumped water to flush at a Hare Krishna temple in Utah (after a deadly microburst knocked out the electricity and almost propelled llamas through the windows when another 78-year-old, this time British, with an infected foot and a cane waving in the air while shouting "We need to get solar power!") and in the High Desert of California (complete with scorpions).

I thought it couldn't get worse than the "situation," shall we call it, that happened at the tiny home on the non-profit farmstead where I pilot-tested *Round America with a Duck* (where I rode my bike around Mableton, Georgia one day with excrement in a bag in search of a dumpster), *but then it did.*

My journey ran March 20, 2023 through August 30, 2023. The very first farm workstay in an old trailer on a repurposed tobacco farm (now a goat farm) came with no port-a-potty, as had been promised in their WWOOF (Working Worldwide on

Organic Farms) online profile. I almost quit (as I almost did other times during the journey, most notably at the next planned farm workstay in Joplin, Missouri), but it was only *Day Two* of the entire trip, and damn, how pathetic would *that* have been.

So I dug deep for inspiration and remembered my neighbor Alan, who hiked the Appalachian Trail (AT). I chose three weeks of digging cat holes outdoors and the howls of coyotes over a shared bathroom practically in the family's living room *that had no door* (just a curtain). If thru-hikers on the AT and Cheryl Strayed (author of *Wild*) on the Pacific Crest Trail (currently so far away and an impossible-seeming pursuit) could do it, so could I.

And so here we were, a wheelbarrow full of human manure later and the Dominican Sisters of Peace praying for me. *God help me.*

But let's back up. How did I even get in this situation? And with a *duck*?

# 1

## New Kid on the Block

I left gifts for my future self. Food in the freezer. Clean closets. A pile of wood chips spread across my wild garden to squelch its growth for the next five months so it wouldn't eat my husband or our house. And then I took one last look at the place our two daughters grew up, at my comfortable suburban life these past few decades, and I closed the door.

It was a pea-soup foggy morning, the first day of spring, and my husband of 33 years (and counting) dropped me off at a curbside bus stop by an Atlanta transit station before dawn. The video he took of me shuffling away with my borrowed 60-liter backpack, dragging a full bike bag and clutching a sack of clementines to share with strangers, is truly the most pathetic piece of footage I've ever seen of myself.

"There she goes," he said to my 87-year-old mother, two daughters and brother-in-law in the group chat.

We had somehow cooked up this idea as our best way forward after my scheduled Peace Corps Uganda departure of June 4, 2020 got derailed due to the global COVID-19 pandemic and my subsequent CDC Foundation service with the State of Alaska as a communications specialist ended.

These were interesting times. Guns, violence and hate seemed everywhere. I didn't yet know it would also be the hottest year on Earth.

Additionally, I was at my own crossroads — a new empty-nester about to turn 60. You think you get 80 years, but maybe you don't. I had survived a recent hit-and-run while riding my bike just a mile from my home, and I had just had a cancer scare. I felt like I was on borrowed time.

A few months prior, my friend Caryn had given me a rainbow-colored rubber duck that I attached to my bike handlebars. People got noticeably nicer when they saw it, at a time when the very fabric of society was breaking down. I got to wondering if perhaps all it would take to change the world for the better would be traveling at a pace where I could look humanity in the face with a duck that made people smile. Maybe along the way, just for kicks and extra credit, I could also learn some new skills that could be useful in our changing world.

So I created this cross-country journey (I didn't yet know it would end up being 10,000 miles/16,100 kilometers) with the intention to do it as cheaply as the 10-country backpacking trip in Europe my friend Julie and I had taken when I was 21. That meant 20 bucks a day, folks, including everything. Doing a workstay exchange for 18 of the 23 planned weeks as part of the global WWOOF program here in the United States would save me food and accommodations costs. WWOOF has around 1,400 participating hosts in the USA alone. Volunteers exchange 20-30 hours of labor a week for food, accommodations, and the education that happens from working on a farm. I would be helping with goats, alpacas, llamas, chickens and gardens.

Traveling between cities via buses and trains would give me the diverse multimodal experiences I enjoy where I could actually meet people from all walks of life and maybe start to feel hopeful again about humanity. Using my folding bike while at farms and in cities would slash rideshare costs and provide me with the ability to experience local life up close and personal — plus bust my stress, as bike rides always did.

It made sense — and cents. It would (and did), in fact, cost less than if I stayed home at the bottom of the hill in suburbia, where I increasingly felt like I was rotting.

We'd been trip-planning as a spousal team for six months already before that bus-departure morning (and for several years before in preparation for my thwarted Peace Corps departure). We attended a WWOOF online seminar together. "Bison!" we had both shouted out loud when we saw the exciting variety of farm host options. ("What does your husband think?" was the number one question people asked me, by the way. He was fully on board, as I was when he took his version of this journey before the kids.)

I tried hard to add a bison ranch in Montana to my mix, kicked off by a stay with my former Turner Broadcasting boss, Terry, who is the mayor of Bozeman, and his wife, Laura, but it was too early and snowy for the rancher to commit, and I needed commitment at this stage so I could plan the bus and train route. So there would be no bison on this journey (or so I thought).

I had already pilot-tested WWOOFing at a nonprofit farm in the Metro Atlanta City of Mableton 25 miles/40 kilometers away by bike for two weeks, living in a tiny home that I loved (lack of bathroom aside). I pilot-tested taking my folding bike on the bus to Macon, Georgia two hours away. I even attended a kirtan festival of spiritual chanting at the Krishna temple in Atlanta, since I was planning on WWOOFing at a Krishna temple in Utah, which has the largest llama rental herd in that state, if you can believe it.

Video calls and texting would mean my husband and family would get to experience all of this with me, and it could breathe new life into our relationships. Note to anyone thinking of doing something like this: You are not leaving your loved ones. There are so many fun ways for them to be involved. Literally every one of my relationships is better today because of having taken this journey. Plus, did I mention my husband and mother started their own routine of going out to lunch together every two weeks?

Just like that senior year of college when I couldn't get my nose out of the *Let's Go Europe* book, I spent endless hours researching my five-month adventure. I contacted dozens of farms, ranches, gardens, and eco-spirituality centers. It was a mind-bending puzzle getting the WWOOF hosts and bus/train schedules to work while taking me from ocean to ocean so that I could dip my bike tire in both the Atlantic and the Pacific, as is tradition on a cross-country journey.

And then there were the packing concerns. I had never camped, if you don't count those couple of random nights in the backyard when the 'possum spooked me enough to retreat indoors, so I didn't have all the handy things that folks who rough it regularly have. I certainly couldn't afford the options in the high-end outdoors shops on the budget I had determined for this journey. I carefully researched and bought all-weather shoes, a travel pillow, and sun-protection clothing. I even got super greens gummies for travel days when I couldn't get enough veggies, as I was concerned about my nutrition while traveling around a country that, in general, doesn't value it.

My friend Brad gave me what turned out to be the MVP of the trip: a sun hat with wide brim coverage and a reflective top that would, indeed, go head-to-head with the numerous sweltering days I was soon to face. My friend Janet gave me a large, light scarf with a bike motif on it that I could wrap around my eyes while sleeping on long-distance buses and trains.

My younger daughter gave me shampoo soap, as she knew I was replacing liquid shampoo with that light, long-lasting product for ease of travel. My older daughter made a song playlist for me that ended up carrying me through the journey. My mother slapped a hundred dollar bill in my hand for emergencies as if it were that summer I left her for Europe with no cell phone, no credit card, and no reservations, before the Euro and when the Berlin Wall was still up.

And my husband gave me a second little duck with a bike helmet I painted to match my own, and he wrote me a beautiful note that I vowed to carry throughout the next 165 days until he would one day, hopefully, greet my midnight train back to Georgia.

I had no way of knowing just yet what was ahead, or how close I would come to quitting within the next 48 hours, and many times after that. I just knew— we both did — that I had to go. So I did.

I checked in with the bus driver and lugged my large backpack and heavy bike bag to the opened luggage compartment under the bus. My folding bike weighed 27 pounds/12 kilograms but the addition of the removable back rack, u-lock and steel cable, folding basket, bungee cords, tools and other supplies brought the total of that bag closer to 50 pounds/23 kilograms, the outer weight limit for luggage not considered oversized on the trains and buses I'd be taking.

I had already ruled out one bus company as an option, by the way, because it required a hard case for my bike, which I would then not be able to carry around, as opposed to a soft case that I could roll up and attach to my handlebars after use. As the counter person told me at the USA's main bus company when I visited the Downtown Atlanta station in order to check logistics prior to my pilot-test, "You can bring your folding bike in a plastic garbage bag if you want!"

A global company now owned the national company and my travels would eventually include a connected network of service providers, including local partners. My first and last bus trips were on buses with that global company's name, although I booked them through the national bus company. The "bus" from Provo to Las Vegas ended up being a 17-seat van with a little trailer behind for luggage, including my bike bag (by then, already replaced with a second one because of the holes I ripped in the first one from dragging it), barreling through the Virgin Gorge that straddles Utah and Arizona. That was a doozy.

I was nervous about our country's main bus company, by the way. They say every released prisoner gets a ticket for it. They say luggage gets stolen by thieves that linger at stations waiting for when the luggage compartments get opened. They say your things get snatched on board the bus while you sleep or when you get off to stretch, use a gas station bathroom, or buy some food. There are also occasional news stories of bus drivers falling asleep and buses tumbling over cliffs (or maybe I've imagined that). And despite the bans of smoking or vaping, the buses often supposedly reek of weed. I didn't know if that reputation was deserved or not, or if it extended to the global company and the local partners.

So I did the only thing that made sense. I got in my comfortable reserved window seat, 3D, and took out my plastic ducks so they could look out the window while the sun rose on I-85. And our trip began.

The whole goal of a bus trip became immediately obvious. *Never use the bathroom.* Truth? I thought this was going to be harder than it was. It turns out the bus drivers stop *a lot*. The stops are stressful, however. In fact, that very first stop in Greenville, North Carolina ended with people crying and running.

"You got 20 minutes," the bus driver alerted us as she pulled into a busy gas station. Many people disembarked and headed for the gas station to buy food or use the bathroom. An equal number stood outside the bus and smoked. I used the bathroom (chancing my bag of cashews, protein bars and toiletries beneath the bus seat in front of me getting stolen). I then did a little dance to stretch my legs, not realizing yet that I would end up doing that dance on mountains, prairies, and beaches; at many, many bus depots and train platforms; and in front of incredible street art across the entire United States.

I got back on the bus with time to spare, as did the smokers, when the bus driver suddenly started moving the bus. Passengers still in the gas station came running out screaming to stop, waving their arms, and in one case, dropping to the ground and pounding the pavement crying.

The bus driver slammed on her brakes, opened the door and shouted, "That other bus company's got y'all traumatized! I'm not leaving you! I'm just moving the bus to get gas! You got eight minutes yet!"

Whew. That was close. And I made a note of the harrowed reaction of these seasoned bus riders. Throughout my journey, a common statement bus drivers from that main bus company would make at a rest stop would be, "Be back in 20 minutes. I'm your bus driver, not your babysitter."

It felt infantilizing and ableist to me. People were hustling as much as they could. Lines were often long to buy food. Sometimes there was only one bathroom that worked and its occupant was taking a dump or a sponge bath. Occasionally, a passenger would say that someone wasn't back on the bus yet, and it became abundantly clear to me from that first gas station onward that I needed to make at least one friendly acquaintance on every trip.

I turned to my seat mate and asked, holding up my bag of clementines, "Wanna orange?" Despite being a loner, I learned quickly that survival is a social game.

My friend Judy picked me up at the Durham, North Carolina transportation center. I had unzipped and rolled up my bike bag and snapped my bike into its usable form so that I could use it like a pack llama (which, of course, was yet to come) to carry the rest of my belongings to her little Prius. People watched me do this, and a woman came over to say wow. I didn't yet know that my bike reveal at every bus and train station was going to be a particularly special opportunity to connect with someone. The connections in Wichita, Kansas and Salt Lake City, Utah would be the most poignant. Just wait.

Folded back up, that bike fit everywhere — except in the car of that rideshare driver in Los Angeles who had a full trunk. ("Why do you have a full trunk?" I asked him. He replied, "Because it's my car!" I countered, "But you're a rideshare driver! You have customers with luggage!" We agreed to disagree and I ended up learning right then and there how to take LA's local trains, *with all my stuff*. But I digress.)

Judy had texted me a few weeks prior to ask if I'd be willing to share the planning process for my trip with her book club the night I would be staying at her and her husband's townhouse in Chapel Hill before heading to my first WWOOF farm workstay the next day. I said yes but asked about COVID protocols, as this trip was really my first time out and about in any big way since the pandemic and I had yet to get COVID myself. She said we'd meet outside on the porch.

The actual night I arrived, however, was cold. Too cold for the porch. We flung open a window in the living room instead. There were about 10 women, Judy's husband and one of Judy's adult daughters. This was the biggest unmasked indoor crowd that I had experienced since the pandemic. The women were an absolute joy with such engaging questions and comments and I found I couldn't easily mask myself while sharing and responding. So, despite my three years of habit at this point, I didn't.

It was only Day One of *Round America with a Duck*, however, and I already had visions of having to cut the trip short if I were to come down with COVID. What would happen if I got it farther away from home? Who would take care of me if I needed care? How would I stick with my budget if I suddenly needed 10 hotel nights for recovery?

Later that night, basking in the glow of the joyous evening, I thought about my COVID protocol during the journey and knew I needed to make some decisions. I determined I'd try to always mask in stores and on buses and trains, avoid indoor restaurants, and not go to any concerts, movies or other large gatherings. With the exception of my father's 90th birthday party a month later in New York, I pretty much stuck with this throughout the entire five-month journey. Truth be told, this made it easier to save money along the way as well, although I surely missed out on some special experiences. I found other ways to connect and spend time with people, and I reveled in my time alone. Maybe I didn't mind these rules. So, if your question is can you take a journey that relies on social skills to survive and thrive while still being a loner introvert, the answer is yes.

I sat on a wall outside Judy's home the next morning with all my stuff stacked neatly around me, waiting for Lish, my first WWOOF host (or second, if you include Hillary at my pilot-test farm in Mableton, Georgia five months earlier).

Lish; her husband, Wayne; and their three children lived on a homestead in Cedar Grove, North Carolina on 40 acres/16 hectares of repurposed tobacco land they call Spinning Plates Farm. It was goat birthing season, and I was excited. "The Tin Can" mobile home where I would be staying was freshly renovated and had a port-a-potty right next to it, according to the WWOOF profile. We would be milking the goats and making cheese. What could go wrong?

Lish — a US Navy Veteran — arrived on time and tossed my stuff into the truck's cargo bed, using ratchet straps to hold it in. She was so solid, and I suddenly felt small and weak, all five-foot-one-inch 118-pounds/53 kilograms of 59-year-old me. But I knew I wasn't. I had been training for this.

Actually, I had been training for the Peace Corps up to and throughout my six departure delays, and then just kept going. Carrying huge jugs of water up the hill in my neighborhood. Jumping rope. Roller skating. Riding my bike, of course. And even doing the monkey bars for the first time in, what, 50 years? I could do this. *I could do this. Don't be soft, Pattie. Don't let anything bother you, Pattie. Go with the flow. You got this.* None of this was natural for an anal-retentive Virgo.

We ran some errands, and it was fun to see the local shops she frequented. One even had a sign out front that said, "Local bison." I laughed out loud. I was originally going to go all the way to Montana to see bison. As a vegetarian, I wasn't going to eat their meat, of course, but seeing them would be cool. Who knew there were bison in North Carolina?

Conversation was comfortable — invigorating, even — as we drove down a gravel road, the white farmhouse appearing like in a storybook. A dog named Peanut ran up to greet us. Children climbed a hay stack.

There was also tons of junk and garbage, but I took that as last fall's leftovers still lingering as winter loosened her grip. I was the first WWOOFer of the year, and there'd be cleaning up, and starting up, to do. I could see where and how I was needed right away, and that was helpful. It was, perhaps, a level of job security, so to speak, I hadn't really had in years, my daughters grown and elsewhere now and my career pretty much in the toilet.

Speaking of toilet, *where was it?* I asked this right away as we walked toward The Tin Can.

"Oh, we got rid of it," Lish replied.

*Got rid of it?* I thought incredulously.

*I didn't ask enough questions. I didn't ask enough questions,* I silently lambasted myself over and over again, thinking about the texts and chats Lish and I had had. I took the WWOOF profile at face value, realizing that the kids I saw were several years older than what was mentioned in the profile. It suddenly hit me — that profile was written before the pandemic!

When Lish opened the door of the Tin Can, I could see immediately that it was not ready for habitation, but there was potential there, if I could just stay open-minded. There were even signs, including a well-organized book case, that it had once been loved.

*No judgment. No judgment,* I reminded myself over and over during these first critical moments. Lish was nice. Peanut was nice. The kids were nice. Nice people and animals don't just happen, and they are more important than nice things. *Hang in there,* I said inside my head. *This place is worth it.*

I asked about the goats who were expecting babies, having harbored some idea that we would be on call day and night for the exciting dramatic delivery of an ongoing number of spring babies.

"They've all been born," Lish replied.

Oh.

No bathroom. No birthing.

And then I met the goats, cows, chickens and cats. All nice, nice, nice, nice. In fact, the animals were so nice that Lish told me that she takes a daily Goat Walk through the extensive woods with them. Would I get to go on a Goat Walk? I suddenly knew I needed that experience in my life, and quitting would deny that opportunity to me. What else would I miss if I quit? Intrigued, I persevered.

So, lack of bathroom and goat births aside, I knew I was where I was meant to be. *Trust the journey, trust the journey*, I said over and over to myself, my mantra. As we walked beneath a fully-blooming apple tree, I snapped off a branch. It took me two hours to transform my living space into something quite lovely. I stuck the branch in a glass jar and placed it on the windowsill in the trailer right above the desk I could use for writing. I felt like I was home — at least for now.

I then discovered the shared family bathroom, to which I had access, was practically in the living room and *had no door*, just a curtain. I'll admit to some trepidation the first time I took a shower, the cats running under the curtain, the children just steps away watching television. *I can do this*, I told myself. *I can do this.*

I simply couldn't use it for doing my business, however. With lots of woods not far from my trailer, I knew I could dig what hikers call cat holes. And so I did. I even marked my spot after I dug it each evening with a pretty garden sculpture that I had found, in preparation for the morning so I could find it, if needed, in the dark, and to give myself some little dash of dignity.

Yes, the first early morning, under moon and stars and the howls of coyotes, scared me. But then I got used to it. It's funny how that works. I even washed my face and brushed my teeth each day outside using water from my water bottle and my purple microfiber towel. To those of you hiking the Appalachian or Pacific Crest Trails: *I get it*. I realize perspective matters. I wrote these notes to myself:

*Don't make a big deal over things that are not a big deal.*
*Practice radical non-judgment.*

Could I have learned two better lessons on just Day Two?

Oh, and there was another message embedded in my head: *Don't quit*. Even when the cows were screaming nonstop that first night (turns out the mama and baby were accidentally separated by a fence) and when flames came out of the propane heater so I turned it off. No need dying in a fire when I wasn't even in fire country yet. I snuggled as deeply as I could in the parachute-material sleeping bag I had brought as a base level, underneath the thick sleeping bag Lish had dug out for me from the back of a shipping container.

That next morning, I tapped into Amazon, ordered a space heater that was the same as the one I have at home, which I call Smiley and which I had gotten after enjoying a space heater at the tiny home where I did that pilot test in Mableton, Georgia. I considered it an act of God that it would be delivered *that very evening* right here in the middle of nowhere. Under the stars on the gravel road, I waved my arms and shouted *yes, yes, yes* when the Amazon driver came rambling down with Smiley. Small victories!

And then it rained. Buckets. A toad-strangler. It didn't seem like it would stop raining, and sure enough, many of the days during the three weeks I was there were wet — which made digging the cat holes easy, but also made me worry about what might be unearthed and float away!

Lish's husband Wayne worked airplane-flights-away as a production rigger for concerts several days every week and Lish had an off-farm part-time job in tiny Hurdle Mills, North Carolina a few days a week. There were simply not enough hours in the day for Lish to run this 40-acre/16-acre farm and family alone.

I had raised my own two daughters while working full-time and tending a large garden but I had a husband who came home every night and I didn't have goats, cows, chickens, cats and a dog. Her mom helped watch the kids while Lish worked, but the juggle and struggle each day was real.

After seeing the situation up close and personal, I decided I would spend two hours a day washing dishes and doing laundry inside the house, as that was clearly a big need of this family, but I was here to farm and wanted to make sure I didn't get stuck inside.

So I donned my rain boots and a bright red thrifted rain jacket and headed on out there, day after day, shovel in hand. I had discovered two significant ways I thought I could make a measurable difference: help Lish plant the large kitchen garden, as it was time for that and it was an overwhelming task for her to do alone; and plant two dozen fruit trees, which were just sitting there waiting to be planted and were going to miss their window of opportunity if much more time passed.

I listened to Lish when we worked and ate together so I could figure out what the to-do list for the farm looked like in her head. I then jotted these actionable items down on a paper plate and stuck that on the refrigerator with a magnet. We marked things off when completed. This became our go-to point of reference to be sure we kept moving forward.

Lish seemed to appreciate my ability to structure my time and get things done, weather be damned. I think perhaps all any of us want to be in life is necessary, and I felt necessary.

I especially loved errand-running with her, as I got to see the rural community and meet her friend Jenny. Jenny is a fellow goat farmer, with whom Lish shared the Hurdle Mills job, each working a few half-days a week, and with whom she castrates and de-horns goats (and yes, I got to witness this). I saw my first peacock at Jenny's farm, not yet knowing what surprise was in store for me at the Hare Krishna temple three months later.

I also had the opportunity while we were driving in the truck to talk with Lish about her past and her dreams for the future. A nuclear power specialist in the Navy for 12 years, she'd lived all over the world, spoke several languages, was a stunning multicultural chef, and was basically a nice, smart, kind, and interesting person. She just wanted their farm to be where her kids grow up close to the land, and then have a place to come home to throughout their lives. That's all. Was that too much to ask for?

Talked out and worked out, I needed my time alone. We're all different about boundaries, and the hours I'd already spent on WWOOF profiles reading comments and reviews made it clear that some people liked to be all-in, spending every waking moment with their hosts and their families, doing anything and everything that needed doing, eating all meals together and socializing day and night. That wasn't me, and, in fact, a lot of hosts don't like that either. I tried to choose places where that didn't seem to be the priority.

I drew firm boundaries as to when my daily hours started and ended and kept track of them religiously. I then spent the rest of my time exploring, relaxing, riding my bike, researching and writing. That dog Peanut ran alongside me every day when I rode my bike up and down the gravel road, the golden grasses swaying in the old tobacco field beside us, which turned out to be one of my most beloved memories of my whole journey.

I also discovered old tobacco drying sheds and was thrilled to find out that some of them across the state were being repurposed for drying hemp, which is a miracle crop making a comeback in limited trials throughout the United States, including here in North Carolina.

Hemp can be used as both a fiber and food, and was in fact encouraged by the US Government to be grown by farmers during World War II so that it could be used to make ropes needed on military ships. The farm right next to Lish's farm was participating in a hemp trial. The closest I came to seeing it was when the cows escaped there, but they came back too quickly, so I missed out. Too bad. It's all very top secret, apparently, and I was definitely intrigued. Stay tuned — I would find out more about hemp later in my journey, in the most surprising of places, and I would even almost get banned from TikTok for posting about it.

TikTok itself almost got banned in the United States while I was at this farm. I posted my little day-in-the-life videos on that booming social media network and was slowly growing a small following, so this dismayed me. I increasingly got breaking news from TikTok, sometimes hours or days before it would turn up in mainstream media, and I valued this insight at a time when every day seemed like there was a new shooting, war, or climate crisis. Plus, I enjoyed the dance trends and other lighthearted content during a time in our country and world when very little felt light. I was especially excited that people, more than ever, were connecting in ways that could truly change the world for the better, and I was concerned that this growing voice was going to be silenced.

The TikTok ban seemed to blow over, and I eventually posted hundreds of videos throughout the journey that were viewed by many people — including my daughters, husband, brother-in-law, friends and mother (for whom I cross-posted on Instagram). It became a fun pursuit each day to capture little moments and then edit, add music and share. If not for TikTok, I wouldn't have done my little dance in front of an old tobacco shed, at the base of a New York City bridge, in the middle of a dirt road in Kansas and on the shore of the Pacific Ocean.

And, you know what? Making those videos made me feel better. They made me laugh out loud. They gave me something creative to do. They serve as a record of my journey. And they often caused me to meet nice strangers both in person and online and have really memorable connections, especially across generations, which is no small achievement in today's society. Maybe TikTok will still get banned, but I was very grateful for it during my journey.

So, it all sounds pretty rosy, right? I sucked it up about the bathroom. I made my home nice. I liked the people and the work. I got to ride my bike. I created my little videos. I even got to go on a Goat Walk with Lish and some other folks (and a cow), and it was indeed marvelous.

But then the gloomies hit. The self-doubt. The ennui. The questions. *What the hell was I doing? What was I hoping to gain from all this?*

There was an old, rusty Cafe du Monde coffee can that I passed over and over again in the little greenhouse. It caught my attention every single time and stirred these mixed thoughts. My itinerary included a visit to Cafe du Monde, the famous coffee and beignets shop in New Orleans, on the very last day of my five-month journey during my overnight in that city when I was scheduled to switch trains for the final leg back to Atlanta. I had originally planned to spend all night between trains at Cafe du Monde asking people if they felt hope, and if so, for what.

I wondered if I would actually make it that far on this journey without quitting or dying, and if so, what did *I* hope for? What did I want to change about myself or my life or the world? Would I do some good, or at least shine a light on others doing so? Would agents rush to represent me for this book, and beg me for a sequel so I could do things like this at farms around the world? Would I become a TikTok celebrity during this trip and thus create a whole new career for myself? Would I inspire someone to make a change in their life, or maybe even save one?

My original concept for this journey was solid but sanctimonious. I had told myself that I wanted to shine a light on our last remaining persistent hope and unsung heroes in a country-at-a-crossroads and world-in-crisis. That I wanted to see climate impacts up close and personal so I could write about them in a more informed way, perhaps as part of the upcoming climate and public health corps with the CDC Foundation (for whom I loved working the past year). I also wanted to learn more resiliency skills that could be helpful in the challenges we are facing as a society. Plus, I had written what's called an aspirational obituary years ago that imagined my life at its end, and there was something on it I planned on doing during this journey.

My husband said, "You know, you *can* just have an adventure. You don't need to prove anything, teach anyone or produce anything as a result."

Having that freedom to *just be* helped, but I didn't want to *just be*. I was turning 60 years old near the end of this journey, if I survived, and somehow there felt like there was more to this experience than just existing through it, even if I simply focused on enjoying it. There was more to *life*, and to my purpose here on Earth. But what?

I wasn't unhappy with my life. I wasn't running away from anything. Sure, I was frustrated that I hadn't been more successful in some ways that were important to me, and I did feel increasingly invisible as an aging woman, but I felt powerful as well, especially as a seed-planter, metaphorically and literally. Our beautiful children were now grown and productive in the world. The many gardens my friends and I had started were still going strong all these years later. My prior published writing shared timeless tips about all aspects of sustainability. *I had done my job.* I could just relax, couldn't I?

No. I could not. But *why* not?

I had bought a sweatshirt to wear on buses and trains that said:

*Dear person behind me,*

*The world is a better place with you in it.*

*Love, the person in front of you.*

I thought that would be a great message for people whose paths I crossed who might need to hear that. On the front of the sweatshirt, it said *You are enough.* I put the sweatshirt on and immediately knew that front message was for *me.*

*I am enough.*

But did I really believe that?

Do *you* believe that about yourself?

This was all much harder than I was letting on, mostly because at the very core of this farm workstay experience, you have to let go of life as you know it, and as a grown-ass woman who had my own home, gardens, and family for 30-something years, it was a challenge. Plus, I chose to preserve the dignity and privacy of both my hosts and myself throughout the journey, so I couldn't share everything I was experiencing with the world — the good, the bad, and the ugly — no matter how much that might boost my meager TikTok views.

After two very full weeks, I needed to see a loved one in person to bounce my thoughts off, kind of like when they do the Loved Ones Visit on the reality TV show *Survivor* (to which I applied, by the way, during one of my delays waiting to leave for the Peace Corps). Judy to the rescue! Having kicked off Day One of this journey with me and then taken photos out her window when Lish picked me up, Judy sensed how vulnerable I felt when we talked on the phone.

She picked me up on a Sunday morning and we went to get coffee and muffins in a hip little town named Hillsborough. We then walked on a lovely path along the Eno River. As luck or God or kismet would have it, we passed graffiti that said exactly what I needed to hear at that precise moment: *All things are difficult until they are easy.*

I needed that.

On one of my last evenings at Spinning Plates Farm, I was walking back from my speedy shower in the family farmhouse all clean and fresh and ready for my private evening reading and writing. You know the feeling — I was *done*. And then Wayne drove past me with his truck full of enormous round hay bales, like the one I had seen when I first arrived and that the cows and goats eat from every day — Bermuda or fescue, or alfalfa for the nursing mamas, in addition to the unlimited amount of fresh forage grazing they do plus some occasional supplemental feed.

We crossed paths and I asked the question I sometimes ask my hubby when I don't really want him to answer yes but it would be polite to ask. You know the one.

"Can I help you?" I dared.

Wayne replied, "Do you want to learn how to drive the tractor?"

Drive the tractor? I had never done this. I was about to leave this farm. I didn't know if I would ever get to do this again. And this would clearly be no help to Wayne — he could move those bales off of the truck with the tractor faster and better than I could. This busy man who spent half of every week traveling and working elsewhere was offering to teach me *just for my own sake.*

Of course I said yes. Wayne even offered to take a video of me operating that machine, lifting those enormous hay bales, moving them precariously and dropping them accurately where they needed to go. That experience turned out to be among my favorite from the entire journey. From that day on, I never shied away from wanting a yes when I asked those four risky words: "Can I help you?"

Wayne was also the very first person of the journey to sign the duck hat. My friend Brad had given it to me, along with that great sun hat. It was a cover for my bike helmet that looked like a bright yellow duck. I didn't see myself wearing it, but I did know a better use for it.

One of my very favorite books is titled *Round Ireland with a Fridge*. It's the memoir of a comedian who lost a bet and then had to hike around the perimeter of Ireland with a refrigerator. So many generous and joy-based things happened along the way, and he asked people he met to sign the fridge. I always wanted to do some kind of journey like that and wondered when and how. *Round Georgia with an Aquarium* just didn't seem to gel for me. But when Caryn gave me that duck and I saw how people reacted to it, the title for my journey wrote itself. Brad's duck hat could be my refrigerator. My hosts along the way could sign it.

After Lish signed it as well, I tucked the duck hat into my backpack and strapped the sun hat to the outside of it, along with my little duffles holding my travel pillow, sleeping bag and hammock.

My dad, about to turn 90 years old, always sang Willie Nelson's "On the Road Again" whenever he packed up to leave our home during all the times he and my stepmom visited over the years. They hadn't been able to come down for 10 years now, not since my older daughter's high school graduation, but that song still rang in my head every time I prepared to leave somewhere. I set up my camera and made a TikTok, accompanied by that song, as I would whenever I left anywhere I stayed throughout the journey.

Judy, her husband and younger daughter got to sign the duck hat next when I circled back to them for a night before catching a train to Philadelphia. After a few hours riding my bike around Chapel Hill (and realizing, ohhhh, that's why the word hill is in the city's name), and another lovely dinner, I packed my bag, did my little "On the Road Again" twirl, took photos of fun leaps in the air with Judy on the train platform, and boarded the once-a-day train heading north.

As I settled into my window seat — my bike bag and backpack safely stored as luggage and my snack bag full of nuts, protein bars, and a fresh bag of oranges at my feet — I watched North Carolina and Virginia slip by. I never napped. I never read. I just stared out the window, watching all the hellos and goodbyes as people boarded and exited at the tiny train stops along the way, often moving me to tears. How beautiful people can be. How much love there is in the world. How grateful I felt to be alive.

I was wearing my sweatshirt and glanced down at its message to me. *You are enough.* The last 10 years had taken me to the edge several times, most recently the prior Christmas. Although up-tempo and optimistic by nature, I was not immune, however, to the personal and societal effects of global challenges. The pandemic. Job insecurity. Rising costs. Road violence. Gun violence. War. And mostly, for me, climate change.

As a gardener ever since the tragedies of 9/11/01, when planting a seed seemed like the only act of faith in the future I could take, I had seen up-close-and-personal the climate impacts in my region and the lack of meaningful action to combat them as a society.

I had also learned and wrote a ton about Alaska for my job the prior year, specifically how they are experiencing three times the rate of climate impact as the rest of the USA. A significant report I read about Alaska's current dire situation even introduced me to the word solastagia, originally coined by an Australian philosopher named Glenn Albrecht and increasingly used to describe a grief and mourning for a lost way of life due to climate change.

*Solastagia*. That's what I felt.

I asked Chat GPT what had changed in the environment just since I was born almost 60 years prior in 1963. Here's what it said, with its disclaimer that these are rough estimates and actual statistics may vary slightly depending on the source of data:

* Global temperature: The Earth's average surface temperature has risen by about 1.2°F (0.7°C) since the late 1800s, with the majority of this warming occurring since the mid-20th century;

* Carbon dioxide ($CO_2$) concentration: The concentration of $CO_2$ in the atmosphere has risen from about 315 parts per million (ppm) in 1963 to over 414 ppm in 2021. This increase is primarily due to the burning of fossil fuels, deforestation and land-use changes;

* Ozone depletion: The ozone layer, which protects the Earth from harmful ultraviolet radiation, has been depleted by human-produced chemicals, particularly chlorofluorocarbons (CFCs). The Antarctic ozone hole, which forms each spring, has grown larger in area and longer in duration over the past few decades;

* Biodiversity loss: Many species of plants and animals have become extinct or are at risk of extinction due to human activities such as habitat destruction, pollution, and climate change. According to World Wildlife Fund (WWF) Living Planet Report 2020, the world has lost around 68% of the world's wildlife since 1970;

* Deforestation: Large areas of forest have been cleared for agriculture, urban development, and other human activities, leading to loss of biodiversity and carbon sequestration, as well as increased greenhouse gas emissions. Since the 1960s, an estimated 5.2 million square kilometers (2 million square miles) of tropical forests have been destroyed;

* Water scarcity: Many regions around the world are facing increasing water scarcity due to over-extraction of groundwater, pollution, and the impacts of climate change;

* Plastic pollution: Plastic waste is a serious problem, affecting the oceans, marine life, and coastlines around the world. An estimated 8.3 billion tons of plastic has been produced since the early 1950s, with about 60% of that plastic ending up in landfills or the natural environment.

Ouch.

I did what I could — riding my bike as my primary transportation, eating a vegetarian diet for 15 years now, growing food and helping others to do so, staying involved with my local city (which I had done since it first became a new city 14 years prior) on issues relating to triple-bottom-line sustainability, applying to the Peace Corps to help elsewhere — but I felt it was never enough. *I* was never enough.

I couldn't do it alone, and forward progress was so small to not even matter sometimes. Did *I* even matter? Was I wasting my life on Sisyphean pursuits to make a difference that would never ripple beyond my backyard? Even *in* my backyard, I had experienced a 95% loss of pollinators due to circumstances beyond my control. In the dark of night, it was often hard to shake *my* growing solastagia. It was hard to not feel useless, and this feeling lingered inside me and surfaced frequently, including as I gazed out that train window.

Unbeknownst to me just yet, in Washington, DC at that precise moment, someone else was close to ending their life — and our paths were about to cross.

# 2

## Rocky Steps and Groovy Bridges

The seats on the train, two on each side with no middle seats, were so large and roomy that I could stick out my legs straight in front of me while reclined. Power outlets meant my devices were always fully charged. Plenty of places to check out and hang out made it inviting to get up and stretch my legs, including to the café car; the dining car; and, on some trains, the panoramic viewing car with large glass windows and swivel seats that put you up close and personal with your passing surroundings (although that wasn't until I got out West). Bathrooms were plentiful and sometimes varied in their size and offerings. In short, it was lovely.

This particular trip was extra comfortable because my seat mate spent the majority of the journey working on her laptop in the café car, so I had the whole row to myself.

Until the delay in DC.

She returned when the train stopped moving for an extended period of time, and, frankly, I was grateful for her company by then.

It was dark out and I was nervous about getting into Philadelphia at night as a woman alone, and a little chat would ease my anxiety.

We both knew that the train could be suddenly delayed by a freight train, as the freight companies own the tracks and get priority. I did a little online search, however, and discovered that our current delay wasn't goods on their way to market or construction supplies or coal. A person on the tracks had "made contact" with a train and all service was halted. I took that to mean a possible act of suicide. We sat there in the DC station for two hours. Any temptation to complain about a schedule interrupted when a *life* had just been ended would have been heartless. So I didn't.

Instead, my seat mate and I talked during that entire delay. Her destination was Philadelphia also, which was home to her. She worked as a musician with Opera Philadelphia, which I found fascinating as she shared how that organization, like many, was undergoing some big changes. *There are so many ways to live a life*, I thought to myself. And yes, life was *worth* living.

During those final two hours into Philly, I just sat there and thought about lives. Lish on the farm and my musician seat mate were living such different lives. I thought of a conversation I had prior to leaving home with my friend Donna, a US Navy Veteran like Lish. Eight years ago, she dropped her son off at college . . . and then just kept going. She lived out of her car for a year while volunteering all over the United States — tending trails on public land, staffing gift shops, leading teams and being of service in so many other really interesting ways during her Navy retirement. Her travels took her to a Sierra Club assignment in Maine, where she met a guy from New Jersey, who had shown up on his motorcycle.

They fell in love over the bonfires, started traveling together in an RV, and got married. When I left home on my journey, they were living rent-free as docents on a small wild island in Florida maintained by Disney that serves as conservation land as required as mitigation for its expansion.

I had recently talked with my friend Mike, a heart failure survivor and author of multiple books who fell in love with fruit trees and started planting them all over his property — and his city. He branched out (so to speak) to create an intern program where high school students learn how to plant, prune and proliferate the presence of fruit trees in their communities. When his interns recently advocated at city hall for a more fruitful community, he smiled contently. He had passed on the passion.

Donna has wings. Mike has roots. The world is filled with opportunities, folks, just waiting for you to experience . . . or to create. And there are new ways forward right where you live. As a Diana Ross song I loved while growing up in the 1970s asked: *Do you know where you're going to? Do you like the things that life is showing you? Where are you going to? Do you know?*

As we rolled into Philadelphia's beautiful 30th Street Station, I was grateful for this time with this stranger, and with myself. There would be other trains and buses. There would be more time for deep thoughts.

Right now, it was time to look for the helpers, I told myself, channeling my inner Mr. Rogers. I got my backpack and bike bag at baggage claim and snapped my bike open to carry my belongings to the rideshare pick-up location. My driver arrived, I folded up the bike again, loaded up the trunk, and settled in for the ride to the hostel I had booked for the night. I would be spending the next night with my friend Mindy at her home across the river in New Jersey and I had asked her if she wanted to stay with me in Philly this night. She liked to ride bikes, too, and I thought she might want to explore the city with me a bit in the morning.

"In a hostel?" she asked, skeptically.

"Yes! I didn't do the dorm-style room because of COVID concerns, so I have a nice private room! Do you prefer the top or bottom bunk?"

"Um, I'll pick you up tomorrow," she said. "What time is check-out?"

Okay, so hostels aren't for everyone. I had stayed in many while backpacking around Europe when I was 21, from a houseboat on a canal in Amsterdam to a converted convent in Italy. I had stayed in one right before COVID spitting distance from Boston Common in Boston, in a dorm-style room, when visiting my younger daughter at college, and I loved it. It was clean and comfortable and I felt like I had a surprising amount of privacy in my little nook. There were plenty of shared bathrooms, and the common areas were cheery and inviting, *and* there was free breakfast, all much cheaper than a regular hotel would be.

This private room at the hostel in the Old City neighborhood in Philly was a definite upgrade for me from that. But *getting* to the room was its own adventure.

It was close to midnight when the rideshare driver pulled down the alley where the hostel was located and then stopped at the address. My husband was tracking me online (which ended up to be a blessing by the time I got to New Orleans four months later, by the way). Apprehensive, I asked the driver to wait until I got in the door, which he did. A clerk was still at the front desk, for which I was grateful because I know many hostels don't have a person there to greet you after hours. He welcomed me and told me my room was on the third floor. My bike was already snapped open and held my loose stuff in its basket, and my backpack was on me, as I asked him where the elevator was.

"Oh, we don't have an elevator," he replied, smiling impishly. "We have something to help you, however."

*Oh, this should be interesting,* I thought.

"Just go through that door and you'll hear it," he replied.

Intrigued, I hobbled over to the door, opened it awkwardly and shuffled my stuff through it. Inside was a long, narrow staircase. I didn't see an electric chairlift or anything else I was imagining could be helpful.

But then I heard it. The theme from *Rocky*, the 1970s movie that was filmed right here in Philly. This struck me as funny, and I smiled, realizing I faced a choice. Admit defeat, or embrace the challenge.

I breathed deeply. Then, I summoned my internal Rocky Balboa, picked up my bike and ran up those stairs. At the top of the first staircase, I laughed when I saw a poster from the *Rocky 2* movie. Intrigued and inspired, I kept running. Sure enough, the third floor had one from *Rocky 3*. Victorious, I threw up my arms in triumph. I may have even shouted, "Yo, Adrian!"

When I got into that bunkbed, I wrapped Janet's bike scarf around my head, covering my eyes to shut out the streetlights outside my window, and I crashed.

I had earned it.

I woke up thinking of one thing and one thing only. The real *Rocky* steps. They were just a few miles away at the Philadelphia Museum of Art, so I carried my bike down the hostel (hostile!) staircases and headed on out.

Philadelphia was beautiful that morning. Crisp and bright, kind of gritty (which I like), filled with art and both old and modern buildings. Lots of bike lanes and paths. The cherry blossoms were blooming, as they had been in Macon, Georgia two months prior when I road-tested taking the bus from Atlanta to there and back one day, and as they had been while I was in North Carolina.

I had a wonderful muffin made of millet at a place named Green Street Coffee Company on Spruce Street, which unfortunately had a ghost bike across the street from it. That's a bike painted white and left locked to a pole as a memorial to a person on a bike killed by a person driving a motor vehicle. Reminded of how vulnerable I was on a bike, I then rode separated from motor vehicle traffic on the Schuylkill River Trail (I still don't know how to pronounce that) to the museum.

There was a statue of Rocky Balboa outside the museum, and a billboard that said "Welcome to Philly" included a visual of him with his arms up in victory. I did my little dance in front of it and tossed up my arms as well for a selfie. I then joined the dozens of other people who were running up and down the museum steps, grateful that I had the physical fitness to do so. A familiar freedom raced through my body — the freedom to be a 59-year-old woman showing up in spaces like hostels traditionally thought of for youth, and taking up space in public when we are supposed to be invisible. Philadelphia freedom, I suppose, as the Elton John song by that name says.

I paused at a skatepark on the way back and took photos of Disco Duck and his little side duck next to a large painted duck on the ground. After returning to roller skating during the second year of the pandemic for the first time since I was a teenager, it felt weird to have recently hung up my skates. I knew, however, that a rib injury (which both my friend Caryn and I had gotten from skating falls) would derail my journey.

I wondered if I would still be able to skate when I got back home, and if I would still want to. Had I skated for the last time in my life already and I didn't even know it? It's like when we brush our children's hair for the last time or read a book out loud to them at bedtime not knowing it would be our final time doing so, that they would be doing it themselves from then on and it would now be just a part of our history.

History surrounded me in Philadelphia, and signs commemorated all of it. When I popped in to the post office in Old City, I discovered where Ben Franklin lived, walked and worked. I thought back to the sweet pony-express-like tiny building in Hurdle Mills, North Carolina, where I had just mailed notes to my family a few days before when I went with Lish to her off-farm job as a greasy spoon cook and convenience store cashier. I realized while traveling across the country that post offices were going to tell their own story about America.

This one was the only colonial-preserved post office in the United States. It even had a museum. As such, it was the only operating post office in the country that did not fly the American flag — because it not yet been created when Ben Franklin was named Postmaster General!

As for flags, I saw them everywhere and took photos and videos with my ducks by them. Our American flag has become a symbol of so much, good and bad, and has even divided our country as to who can claim a right to it. Little by little, I felt like I was reclaiming my right to be a proud American in the ways that have meaning for me.

Being able to travel around this country unchaperoned as a woman mattered to me. Even though there are no rules against it, I knew that it is something most people would not recommend and actually considered dangerous or foolhardy right here in the United States. We may not even realize how restrictive we've become as a society, especially with women and girls. No being out at night. No being alone in public spaces, especially parks and mass transportation. So many unwritten rules and de-facto curfews.

If something were to happen to me, the fact that I was a woman traveling alone would make the headlines. It would somehow make me liable for whatever happened to me. If I happened to be wearing something that revealed my body (such as what I wear to ride my bike in the heat), *fuggedaboutit* (as we say in my native New York, where I was heading next).

I realized my freedom — as an American, as a woman — required me to defy that. To throw that in the face of society, and to model a different option for the little girls sitting in the backs of SUVs who always peered at me out there on my bike, often even waving, as they passed. I was a practically-feral child in the 1960s and 70s, going everywhere on my bike, often alone. Many of us were. I was not going to become a caged, cooped-up 60-year-old.

By the way, "Is that safe?" was the third most-asked question I got when people heard about my trip. What a complicated question. I thought about this not long before my journey when I got a mammogram. My mom has already survived two different breast cancers. We know that in addition to family history, so many environmental factors can cause cancer. Breathing, eating, *being* is dangerous. A healthy diet and regular exercise seems to help. So I do that. And then there's COVID. I'm vaccinated. I still mask in public indoors. I try to avoid crowds.

I often strap a three-foot-long foam pool noodle I call BikeNoodle onto my bike in my city. It serves as a traveling bike lane in places that are dangerous-by-design, such as where I live, and has worked miraculously. Except that one time. But I didn't bring it with me on this journey, so that meant I would have to choose my routes extra carefully.

My local police blotter was packed daily with motor vehicle driver charges, by the way, and I expected many communities around the USA were similar. I had dangerous encounters every single day just trying to get to the supermarket or park in the place I call home. *A hero ain't nothin' but a sandwich. A hero ain't nothin' but a sandwich* I chanted to myself often, to remind me to make conservative choices with the only goal of making it home alive.

I cobbled together just a five-mile route by Lish's farm in North Carolina. Anything beyond that had high-speed motor vehicle traffic. I thought I was relatively safe on my little country ride. And then dogs chased me. Not even BikeNoodle would have helped with that!

Walking was no better. Whether in a parking lot or on mass transit, I habitually do the 20 or more things every girl and woman learns to do when we walk out the door. It's so routine at this point it's almost subconscious: the keys between our fingers, our purses cross-body, our eyes darting left and right and constantly looking over our shoulders. We memorize license plates of cars that pass us slowly and lock the doors the very second we get in our own cars. We don't sit and read a book on a bench or take a nap anywhere outside. And we learn to trust our guts.

I additionally knew it was statistically more dangerous for me to stay home and sit on the couch. Obesity, heart disease, diabetes and depression were far bigger killers of women. The average American woman was two inches taller than me and 55 pounds/25 kilograms heavier. Riding my bike daily, as was my habit for years now and which helped me both physically and mentally, probably saved my life in more ways than one.

For the record, I was also afraid of snakes and scorpions and horses that kick and goats with horns and the heat of the desert and tornadoes and floods and maybe even the possibility of joining a cult, and a whole bunch of other things that I expected I'd encounter on this journey.

So, *"Is it safe?"* Actually, probably, no. Nothing is. But I did this journey anyway. And, spoiler alert, I will tell you now, I was scared every single day for 165 days. If you are thinking about doing something that scares you, don't wait until it doesn't or you never will. Do it scared.

Mindy came driving down the alley as I was sitting on the curb in front of the hostel waiting for her. She poked her head in to take a look around and agreed it was nice. "But, no," she added, laughing.

After visiting her younger son briefly, we drove to her home in the largest log cabin neighborhood in the United States. Now, let's back up about Mindy. Mindy is a New Yorker. A city girl. A big laugher, fast talker, smart thinker. To see her in her home in that idyllic neighborhood flipped my impression of her upside down. She loved it there. Private lakes. An annual lantern festival on canoes. Kids riding bikes everywhere (be still my heart). You know someone for 30 years — we worked together at the UPS global headquarters in Atlanta — you think you know them. My overnight stay with Mindy added a whole new level to our relationship.

And *she took care of me.* Like Judy, she had been following my journey to date and knew that I was hungry, tired and vulnerable.

It was another true Loved Ones Visit at a welcoming home where I had a comfortable bed and private bathroom.

We got take-out at a highly-creative chef-driven pizza place, talked deep into the evening on the back porch, took a conversation-laden walk in the morning, and then wandered around a fascinating restaurant named Rats, believe it or not, right next to a 42-acre/17-hectare sculpture garden, where we enjoyed an outdoor lunch (without rats) before she dropped me at the commuter train station. Hugs and tears goodbye, and I was on the road again. Me, Willie Nelson, my bike, backpack and ducks.

This metropolitan area's commuter system has train cars specifically accessible for people with disabilities and with strollers and bikes, so I got to just roll on to it, sit down and relax during the hour or so ride to New York City's Penn Station.

I was heading there for my father's 90th birthday on Long Island. My brother and I were hosting a family party at a nice Italian restaurant right next to my dad and stepmom's condo. I was nervous about this because it would be my first crowded indoor gathering without a mask since COVID, book club meeting in Chapel Hill aside. I had somehow made it three years without getting the virus, and my whole trip depended on that streak continuing. This dinner was especially important, however.

My husband was driving up. My younger daughter, who lived in New York City, was coming via Long Island Railroad, and my older daughter and her fiancé were flying in from Los Angeles. My brother and his son would be driving there from New Jersey, and my stepbrother, his wife and daughters, and his younger daughter's fiancé were all coming from around Long Island.

We had planned to all be together two Christmases before but the surge in the Omicron COVID strain hit New York City hard literally minutes before that holiday and we canceled our trip. I had been heartbroken about it, and so this gathering felt irreplaceable to me. A 90-year-old is no spring chicken (I had already left those at Lish's), and I didn't know if or when we'd ever have this group together again. But I was nervous.

The train arrived at Penn Station and I stood there on the platform watching everyone head up the stairs. I wondered if I should cue that theme song from *Rocky* again, or find an elevator. I found the elevator.

I exited on chaotic Seventh Avenue and just stood there a moment contemplating my next moves. I was heading to my younger daughter's apartment near the East Village for the night in the very same complex, ever so coincidentally, where her father and I had lived 33 years ago, before going to Long Island the next day, and my overloaded bike suddenly seemed like a very big challenge to ride the two miles/three kilometers across Manhattan. I even made a TikTok where I said to the camera, "I may have overestimated my ability to do this, but I *am* a New Yorker — and I don't give up."

I would rewatch that video at several make-or-break moments later in the journey when quitting became a very real option. I couldn't have guessed right then and there in front of Madison Square Garden that I was sending an important gift to my future self, but I was.

Yes, I made it to my daughter's apartment. Barely. Blocked bike lanes caused me to stop short, and the hardest part of riding was getting going again with all the uneven weight on the bike. Delivery guys on fast e-bikes going the wrong direction almost caused me to topple. Checking for traffic over my shoulder was practically impossible with my backpack on. I knew I needed to reconfigure my belongings the next morning if I was going to do this safely. But I was a New Yorker, *and I don't quit.*

What I *did* quit almost a year prior, however, was alcohol. Not that I had a problem — but, to be honest, I wasn't exactly sure about that. What was normal anymore? When I first started thinking about taking some sort of journey, I decided to quit alcohol so I could become as healthy as possible, save money, and see once and for all if I had a problem or just a habit. My mother stopped drinking when I was eight years old, and other members of my extended family had grappled with the disease of alcoholism so it was a legitimate concern of mine. It turns out quitting wasn't hard, so I'm chalking my daily dinner wine up to a habit instead of a problem, although I still had to adjust to a new way of living without it.

I also gave up caffeinated coffee, glutton for punishment that I was. The Krishna temple in Utah where I would be WWOOFing allowed neither alcohol nor caffeine and I didn't want to be going through caffeine withdrawal while on the road. Plus, I figured trying to find coffee while traveling would not only be a bitch but an expense that my 1985-era budget simply could not handle.

So there I was in New York City, alcohol and caffeine free. My sweet daughter rose to the occasion and planned a lovely night out for us that started in a wonderful sober dive bar in the East Village, the first in the nation, named Hekate Café and Elixir Lounge. I chose a drink named The Healer, which came with a sprig of rosemary. My younger daughter chose the Jalapeño Margarita. We moved to an outside bistro table with our drinks and chatted while people-watching before strolling to an outdoor dinner at a Mexican take-out window.

It was the first gorgeous spring night in New York City and spirits (human, not alcohol) were high. The cherry blossom wave I was riding up the East Coast continued with full blossoms right there on 14th Street. We ended the evening perched together on the edge of a colorful fountain chatting under the stars. My cup, as they say, overflowed.

The next morning, I slipped out early so as not to wake my daughter and her roommates and I took a walk around the East Village and what we used to call Alphabet City. Every block had three or four ethnically-diverse community gardens, and I found myself getting excited about the variety of farms, gardens, and other types of WWOOF locations where I would be working coast to coast.

I also passed another ghost bike and made a little TikTok about it, as I had when I saw the one in Philly. After lunch with my daughter, I rode slowly and carefully back to Penn Station, folded up my bike so it would fit easily beside my commuter train seat (no separate bike car available like on the New Jersey train), and headed for my hometown of Mineola just 30 minutes away. The train chugged along, making that familiar rhythmic sound that lulled me into memories and daydreams.

As I got closer to my stop, I realized that for maybe the first time since I moved away from New York all those years ago, my dad would not be at the station to greet me. He was having eye problems and both walking and driving were becoming challenges. I told him I had the bike and it would be easier for me to just ride to his condo less than a mile away. But it hit me — hard — when the doors opened and the bench on the platform was empty.

I woke just before daybreak to the steady hum of motor vehicles on Old Country Road outside my dad and stepmom's condo. The roosters at Spinning Plates Farm seemed so far away. Busy intersection aside, this condo building was special. Deep, unexpected, way-beyond-neighborly intergenerational friendships started during a days-long blackout here in New York years ago when all the neighbors met and ended up sharing their defrosting food.

They've been friends ever since (plus are quick to welcome new people to the building) — cocktails and Christmas parties, cards on Tuesdays and Fridays, and casual conversation and cooperation every day. This one has cancer. That one has the flu. Another one's mother is ill or is having a baby or needs a parking spot or package picked up. They're all ages and walks of life. And they truly love each other.

"We are family here," says Billy, who was running for the Board of Directors of the collection of six buildings that make up this little corner of the world.

I was somehow reminded of an excellent article in *The New York Times Magazine* way back in 2008 about how displaced people are systematically arranged in refugee camps: four-six people make a household, a cluster of 16 households makes a community, 16 communities form a block, four blocks are a sector, and four sectors are a camp. The fact that just 16 households make a community jumped out at me then and made me realize how little it would really take to make a difference where I lived. I started a Sharing

Garden by the curb of my home, which I revived during COVID, and did, indeed, feel like I connected with at least 16 households during that time. That made me feel part of a community.

I thought briefly about that Sharing Garden now 900 miles/1,448 kilometers away and untended. I planted garlic there last fall, knowing it would not need any special care and could be easily harvested by passersby in June. The garden would then lay dormant, or weedy, until I got home and could revive it as what architect Steve Mouton calls a "a gift to the street," when I hoped to be able to plant fall crops and share abundance again.

This weekend, I experienced a different kind of abundance. My husband arrived and it felt like both forever and a moment ago since I saw him. My older daughter and fiancé flew in for literally twenty-four hours, just enough time to celebrate her 28th birthday and her grandfather's 90th. She was our focus at a tapas and wine bar (cranberry juice with lime for me, please) for a nosh of Spanish olives, Shishito peppers, Marcona almonds and hearty bread before my father's party that evening.

I gave my husband an olive and said, "Olive *you*." We were so rich in ways that had nothing to do with budgets, and I was grateful for it. I knew it needed to last me for months until I saw him and my daughters again in Los Angeles, if I were to make it that far. Catching myself for thinking *if* instead of *when*, I reminded myself, "I am a New Yorker, *and I do not quit.*"

I never, not once, passed Long Island's Meadowbrook Parkway without remembering how when I was 15 years old, I was pulled over by a police officer for riding my bike on it. It was my fastest way home, and it made sense to me to ride on it in its wide shoulder. The police officer didn't see it that way. Had I gone just a little farther east to the Wantagh Parkway, I would have found a multi-use path running right alongside it, even back then in the 1970s.

I was shocked, all these years later, to finally ride the Wantagh Parkway Path for the first time in my life and see how wonderful it is. It was built during the biggest bike boom in United States history. Even notoriously car-centric Los Angeles built a bike trail network around that time. I couldn't help imagining what our country would have been like if the positive bike vibes had continued. Instead, it felt like we lost 40 years of forward progress.

I was on my way to Jones Beach to dip my bike tire in the Atlantic Ocean, as is tradition on cross-country journeys by bike (even though I was also traveling by buses and trains). The roundtrip ride at 41 miles/66 kilometers was the longest bike ride of my life. I would beat that record on another highway path 1,800 miles/2,897 kilometers away later on my journey.

Overwhelmed by the beauty of the swaying golden grasses (different from the ones at Lish's farm but I did not yet have the app that could identify them for me) and sounds of seagulls, I taped a quick video message to my friends Janet and Mindy, who are both from Long Island as well, and texted it to them. Janet wrote back:

"I know exactly where you are! My friend Betty and I rode on the actual parkway down to the beach back in 1974 to help promote the building of that path!"

Wow. To think that my friend's younger self helped make this ride possible was pretty cool. What gifts were we sending our future selves, and other people we don't even know or know *yet*, right now? My visits to New York always had me time traveling between my past and present, and it was fun to add this future quality to it. What gifts would I send my future self during this journey? I thought about 21-year-old me, traipsing around 10 countries of Europe, and how often I have drawn strength from those experiences, like gifts from my younger self. I even get excited when my just-one-day younger self leaves me a little piece of chocolate or handful of chips in the cupboard rather than finish them off.

When I got to the ocean, grey clouds were starting to roll in and the wind picked up. There were very few people there, but I did meet an elderly man named Tom who insisted I tell people how important it was to use a brush on your hair, not just a comb, because it stimulates its growth and could help you not lose it as you age.

"Look at my head of hair!" he exclaimed, pointing to its fullness.

He had a point. He did have a very full head of hair.

I suggested, "Why don't *you* tell them?" as I lifted up my camera. He straightened up, looked right into it, and delivered his important message.

So, brush your hair, folks.

My gray and wheat-colored hair blowing every which way, I trudged through the sand down to the ocean, the only soul out there. I leaned my camera against my water bottle in the sand to record this momentous occasion and ran into the ocean. After dipping my front tire in the water, I hoisted my bike over my head, my arms raised triumphantly.

Like Rocky.

I then scribbled my guiding words, my mantra, in the sand.

*Trust the journey.*

I added the ducks to the scene and took photos. Although I was already a month into my journey, this felt like a new beginning.

I looked back at my video when I got to the boardwalk and realized I was supposed to dip the back tire in the ocean at the first side of the country and the front tire in the ocean at the end, no matter which direction you cross (although most people do it west to east across the United States due to the prominent direction of the winds). That is how it's done if you look it up online. I wondered if I should shlep back down there and re-do it.

"No; I'm doing things differently," I told myself. This was *my* journey.

On the way back to Mineola, after eating a celebratory Carvel ice cream cone as the sun reappeared, I stopped short when I passed a mural on the side of a building.

It was of Rocky.

I can't make this stuff up.

*Slow down, you move too fast*
*You got to make the morning last*
*Just kicking down the cobblestones*
*Looking for fun and feelin' groovy*

I sang those words at the top of my lungs as I rode my bike across the 59th Street Bridge, immortalized in a song by Simon and Garfunkel. Also called the Ed Koch Queensborough Bridge, it connected Manhattan's Upper East Side with the borough of Queens across the East River. Despite hundreds of times back in New York, including frequent work visits with Turner Broadcasting after I moved to Atlanta and holiday trips to visit family, I had not ridden my own bike over a bridge in New York since I lived there in my 20s. I had only ridden CitiBike over a bridge — the Brooklyn Bridge — once.

To be riding my own bike, ducks bobbing with each tire rotation, was glorious because I didn't have to worry about switching out the bike at a bikeshare station in time — every 30 minutes — to not incur additional fees. I didn't have to worry about anything, in fact. And so I sang. I sang, and sang and sang.

On the other side of the bridge, greeted by easy-to-access separated bike lanes, I even proclaimed out loud, "This is not your father's Queens!" evoking both a famous Chevrolet car commercial and the fact that my dad had grown up in Corona, Queens. This Queens had changed, and was, in fact, a hotspot for young professionals now. It was suddenly no surprise to me how Queens, listed separately from Manhattan (which has its own great bike infrastructure) earned a place on the PeopleForBikes best-cities-for-bikes list.

As a PeopleForBikes ambassador, League of American Bicyclists Cycling Instructor, first Metro Atlanta Bicycle Mayor as part of a global consortium with the Amsterdam-based social enterprise BYCS, the author of the book and blog *Traveling at the Speed of Bike, and* a road violence survivor, bike access-for-all mattered to me. It was, in fact, something I was specifically going to be checking across the USA during this journey. My Metro Atlanta city was moving forward but very slowly and with endless fighting along the way, so I was curious what the state of the nation truly was, rubber-hits-the-road, on this issue.

I was looking for "wows" and everything counted as I was used to both best-in-class bike infrastructure in the City of Atlanta and next-to-nothing where I lived in my Metro Atlanta suburb city.

So artist-painted concrete barriers protecting a bike lane? Wow. Those little bike lights at intersections indicating when it was safe to cross? Wow. Cleared sight lines and frequent escape routes that made isolated paths safer for women traveling alone? Wow. The multi-use path network through neighborhoods in Chapel Hill, which I rode when I was there visiting Judy? Wow. That car-protected bike lane on 52nd Street that I took cross-town from the Eighth Avenue protected bike lane through the Theatre District to get to the 59th Street Bridge? Wow. The lovely path when I got off that bridge leading to a path and park right along the river? A definite wow. I did, indeed, feel groovy, and I even did my little dance.

Enjoying my outer-borough bike ride so much, I decided to head south to Brooklyn and swing back to Manhattan over the Williamsburg Bridge. This would take me through a neighborhood where I'd never been and which my younger daughter loved. But first, what bridge was this? How could I have lived in the New York City metropolitan area for 26 years of my life and never, not once, have gone over the Pulaski Bridge? What else was around the corner just waiting for me to discover in life?

I rode up and down a few blocks and was so grateful for my ability to travel at a pace where I could explore like this. I knew there would be a day I could no longer ride my bike. Today was not that day.

I passed a cute local book store with a vintage bike locked up at the bike rack in front of it. The bike had a metal basket that just begged for me to leave the first of half a dozen pairs of earrings I had brought with me to share on the journey as part of Free Art Friday, even though it wasn't Friday. (No rules, remember?)

Free Art Friday is a global movement where artists leave little pieces of art out and about in public. They are gifts to the street, in fact. Artists then post a photo of the art in its location as an alert to anyone following the hashtag (often #FreeArtFriday followed by the city's name). Whoever finds it posts a photo indicating it was claimed, and then they get to keep it, although mostly random folks just come across them when they are out walking or riding their bikes so you usually don't find out what happened to them, but it's still fun. I had done it a ton of times in Atlanta with various things I created over the years.

The earrings, however, were a product I made out of used bike tubes and other recycled bike parts that I called BikeBloom. They were on a hang-tag that featured my original painting of a bike with flowers in the basket. As a popular sound on TikTok went, "I know the influence. I know the impact. And I know the vibes. And the girlies love the vibes." BikeBloom was all vibes. It was my way to invite more women and girls, who are underrepresented in public space, into the bike joy whether or not they ever rode a bike. If they did want to ride a bike but didn't know how, I offered two free online classes that I developed specifically for them (which I often gave in person over the years as well). I had their backs.

Back in Metro Atlanta, an art gallery in Decatur, Georgia, the only Silver-level Bicycle Friendly Community in the state, was displaying BikeBloom earrings while I was traveling, and my local REI purchased a batch to sell as well.

I took out a pair of the earrings and dangled them from the basket. I made a TikTok (of course) and went on my way, smiling about it, my own BikeBloom earrings swinging as I rode. I would eventually leave BikeBloom earrings across the country in Oklahoma City (where I wasn't even planning to be overnight, but alas, the journey took me there), Boulder, Salt Lake City and Los Angeles. Maybe you even found them!

On the way back to Penn Station, I approached an intersection while in the 13th Street bike lane. A man in a dapper suit on a Brompton folding bike was right in front of me waiting for the light to change. As I pulled up behind him, he glanced over his shoulder and then exclaimed, "That! That is what I want!"

He was on a much more expensive folding bike than mine, so I wasn't sure what he meant. Intrigued, I got off my bike as he got off his and he said, "I've been wanting to get my bike painted, and I have the vision in my head, but I couldn't explain it to anyone."

He pointed again at my bike. "That! That is what I want!"

I've painted all my bikes with multicolored acrylics. The BikeBloom earrings are painted the same way, as is my bike helmet, and even my roller skates and a pair of my shoes (neither of which were with me on this journey). My bikes often start conversations with people.

Introducing himself as Bernard, he asked if he could commission me to paint his bike. For one brief moment there on the corner of 13th Street and Sixth Avenue, I saw a flash of Famous Artist Pattie painting bikes for celebrities. I saw myself living again in my favorite city, riding my bike over bridges every day. Seeing my father and stepmom and younger daughter whenever I wanted. Lunching with agents about a children's book about this journey from the ducks' point of view, and the subsequent movies! Did my trust-the-journey mantra and all the leaps I did as part of my little dance alone and with friends mean this was a calling I should answer?

I replied in the only way that felt right just then.

"Would you mind saying all that on camera?"

Check my TikToks. You'll meet Bernard. And Tom, for that matter. *Brush your hair.*

Back on Long Island, I locked my bike to the diner railing just as my friend Marcelle pulled up in her car. She and I had met when I was 19 years old as a freshman at the C.W. Post Campus of Long Island University, a short daily car commute from my home, before I transferred and moved upstate to the State University of

New York at Geneseo. We were in a rhetoric class together and often got into lively debates from our seats on opposite ends of the room. After class one day, she waited for me in the hallway. When I walked out, she said, "Hi. I just moved here from Salt Lake City and I don't know anyone. Do you want to go to a movie?"

I said yes.

We became fast friends but then fell out of touch over the years as our lives in different parts of the country consumed us. Now both empty-nesters, we were back together stronger than ever. Very few people understand me as fully as Marcelle does, nor find my quirks as funny as she does. If you've lost touch with a dear friend, consider revisiting your relationship. It is worth it.

Not wanting to part, we took photos of us doing leaps like Judy and I had. We talked there in the parking lot about her meeting me in Salt Lake City later on my journey. She had been wanting to go out to visit her sister-in-law anyway, so this actually might work, she said.

"I have a two-night rental apartment," I told her. "You could stay with me. I want to visit the Great Salt Lake before its final toxic demise."

There was a recent Opinion piece in *The New York Times* about the disappearing Great Salt Lake and the release of mercury, arsenic and much more into the atmosphere. It was a stunningly reported and told story titled *I Am Haunted by What I Have Seen at Great Salt Lake*. I didn't know what I could possibly add to Terry Tempest

Williams' coverage or Fazel Sheikh's photos but that was my plan before heading south from Salt Lake City to my WWOOF workstay at the Krishna temple and llama ranch outside Provo.

"I'll wear my PPE," she deadpanned.

After tapping into online maps to find the safest route, I then rode my bike past the childhood home of the WWOOF host, Elise, with whom I would be staying in Boulder. She actually grew up in the much-wealthier village next to mine! She hadn't seen her childhood home in years and was grateful that I offered to ride by after I shared with her I had passed my own childhood home. At Elise's old home, I took photos and videos and texted them to her. She kind of regretted it, she told me. So many trees had been cut down. Things had changed. Maybe not everything is worth revisiting.

On the swirly, hilly way from Long Island's exclusive North Shore, where Elise had lived, back to modest Carle Place, where I was now staying in a hotel with my husband just a quick mile bike ride to my dad and stepmom's condo in Mineola, I cut through the State University of New York's Old Westbury Campus. A sign I kept passing said HorseAbility and pointed forward, so I kept following it. I wondered if it was a therapeutic horse facility, either for rehabilitating horses or for providing what's called hippotherapy to people with disabilities.

I was always interested in horses because I had ridden horses as a teenager (terribly, often earning the last-place brown ribbon, which meant I had to sit there on the school horse in the ring as every other rider got their ribbon and left). I only took one weekly lesson, funded generously by my parents, and eventually added a second weekly lesson paid for with my McDonald's earnings.

As luck, or shall we say, *muck*, would have it, I worked mucking stalls in exchange for four dollars a day and a free lesson a week the summer I turned 18, an occasion for which my friends gifted me a pitchfork. I made my entire college decision to go to C. W. Post because they had a riding team, which I quit after my first semester because everyone else was so darn good, having grown up with their own private horses.

I also took riding lessons for a few months at Chastain Park in Atlanta on Tuesday nights when I worked at Turner Broadcasting. I rode an old horse named Rooster and was happy just muddling along with him, doing a comfortable canter, hopping low fences. My favorite moments were after the class when I left the outdoor ring and was walking Rooster back to the barn, his warm breath in the chilly night on my cold hands. I think I took the lessons just for those moments.

My job required me to travel all over the country, sometimes weekly, so I ended up stopping the lessons but I was satisfied that I had come back to horseback riding on my terms, and was able to put it to rest. Over the years, I had gone on a couple of trail rides —

an especially memorable one with my husband on our honeymoon traversing a steep cliff and galloping along the Caribbean Ocean, and recently with my husband and younger daughter at an eco-enclave just outside Atlanta named Serenbe. I loved horses, but I didn't necessary feel like I needed to get back in the ring. I was in the ring, The Man in the Arena (as Theodore Roosevelt called it), in other ways at this point in my life. I was my own Rocky.

I was, however, looking forward to my next WWOOF farm workstay a great deal. It was at a horse sanctuary in Missouri and I was scheduled to be there for five weeks, which was my longest planned workstay of the journey. I was originally going to go to an alpaca ranch and eco-spirituality center in Kansas owned by the Dominican Sisters of Peace, with whom I had a very warm and wonderful Zoom call and we were all excited. When trying to book my bus to the closest city to them with a stop (which was still a full hour away), however, I discovered the stop had been suspended recently (and there were no other buses that went there), so I made the heartbreaking decision to pivot. Trust the journey, right?

I had had nice exchanges with the horse sanctuary host, Candida, about my role there. I told her I had some riding experience but it had been years. She wrote back that she needed me to re-start the greenhouse, clean the horse tack (which is the leather riding equipment), and write some grant applications for them. I liked that Candida took my specific skill set, as outlined on my WWOOF profile, into consideration when assigning me tasks. Personally, I was also hoping to be able to spend time with the horses helping grooming, and maybe even riding once or twice, although, frankly, that did make me nervous after all these years.

I would actually be there on Memorial Day, and I knew from online research regarding this impressive sanctuary that they sometimes participated in local events. What if I ended up riding a horse in a Memorial Day parade! Cue the *Rocky* theme! Maybe I wasn't done yet challenging myself.

If I only knew then what was about to happen when I arrived there.

But first, when I got to HorseAbility on the SUNY Old Westbury campus, I asked a woman mucking the stalls what it was all about and she introduced me to Jeanne. Jeanne told me that HorseAbility made the lives of people with special needs better through horseback and driver lessons and encounters. Their herd of 30 horses included retired show, racing, police, party and private horses, including a handful of precious miniatures that visit senior homes and events the way therapy dogs do. After volunteering at HorseAbility herself and with her children for many years, she worked full-time managing around 200 volunteers who helped this very special organization succeed.

While we were talking, a man named Robbie passed by with a small cart attached to a miniature horse named Elf after just concluding lessons with a girl with cerebral palsy. He was a retired harness racing trainer now volunteering at HorseAbility. He told me how much it meant to him to be able to share his passion here.

Turning back to Jeanne, I asked her what gave her hope. She motioned toward Robbie and Elf and replied, "Just coming here each day. It's hard not to feel good."

This was one of the better conversations I had about hope on this journey so far. Many people I asked told me they had none, which caused me to eventually change my question from "What gives you hope?" to "Do you have hope?"

Usually as we talked, the people who said they had no hope would think of something small that made them feel hopeful, even briefly. I didn't force this; it just seemed to happen naturally. Maybe just thinking about hope was the thing that made it suddenly visible to us, lurking as it does in the shadows. A butterfly flits by. A bird chirps. A child laughs in the distance. There's dew. There's a spider web glistening in the sunlight. Those kinds of things. They are everywhere.

Do *you* feel hope? Don't answer. Just sit with it a moment and think about it, but don't feel too bad if you come up short. I wasn't particularly sure I even felt hope, especially after reading dire daily news headlines. I had 30 hours coming up on three different buses between New York City and Joplin, Missouri to think about it.

I did my little "On the Road Again" spin outside the hotel and got in my husband's car. He was returning to Atlanta, and I was heading west. He offered to drop me at the Port Authority

Bus Terminal in Manhattan, just as he had dropped me at the bus stop in Atlanta at the start of this journey. I really do not like being in cars and try to avoid them whenever possible, but this seemed important to spend these last moments together before separating again, and I was grateful for his offer.

Driving in Manhattan is crowded and erratic but we had left in plenty of time. I don't like to rush — ever — which, of course makes me a perfect match for bikes, buses and trains. There would be so many stops on this next leg of my journey, with bus changes in Pittsburgh and St. Louis. I didn't yet know about the middle-of-the-night layover in Indianapolis, during a time I had hoped to be sleeping.

Hubby stopped across the street from Port Authority and we unloaded my motley mix of things. I snapped open my bike, loaded it up with the other small bags including the ubiquitous bag of oranges, and tossed my pack on my back, just like that first morning in Atlanta.

This time, however, it all felt lighter. I stood taller. We laughed. And I sauntered, Beatles-style, circa the *Abbey Road* album cover, across 42nd Street, the lyrics from that Frank Sinatra classic song "New York, New York" — *start spreadin' the news; she's leaving today* — in my head. A quick wave, a blown kiss, and I was off, realizing how much I had already changed.

As I entered the bus terminal, I wondered how much we would both change during this trip. However supportive and connected we currently were, would that enhance our relationship or send us in different directions? There was no knowing. It was, indeed, a risk we were taking.

# 3

## No Horsing Around

*Look for the helpers*, I invoked my inner Mr. Rogers again. A friendly woman at an info counter pointed me in the direction of my bus gate and I made my way there. Claiming my spot on line, I performed the magical transformation of folding up my bike and storing it and its multitude of accoutrements into the black bike bag.

I had glued wheels to the bottom of the bike bag before the journey but they had fallen off and ripped small holes in it already. Moving anywhere with the loaded bike bag involved a great deal of trudging because I could barely lift it up because of my short stature and dragging it would only rip it more. Making a friend was a necessity if I wanted to use the restroom (which, as we know, was critical before getting on that bus and risking having to use the mobile port-a-potty onboard).

So, yes, you know what I did.

"Wanna orange?" I offered the man behind me with the Yankees cap on. He took it, of course (not one person said no to an orange during the entire trip). We got to talking, and once I felt we were truly committed to each other as much as strangers at a bus depot could be, I asked if he'd watch my bag so I could go to the restroom, which he kindly did.

Each encounter with a stranger reinforced the point that resiliency during our tumultuous times is, indeed, a social game. My ability to make connections would matter, and getting better at it on this journey could one day save my life.

I was racking up the new skills. I had already learned, in North Carolina, that being able to squat to do your business was an important skill if I ever had to flee or live outside for any reason. As an aging woman, I would be a burden to others who are fleeing if I could not do this and I would risk being left behind. It would become abundantly clear to me throughout the journey what other skills could be critical, and ways that I could work to strengthen them. They may surprise you when I share them with you.

Watching Manhattan fade outside my bus window reminded me of the last time I saw the Twin Towers, now memorial holes. We were driving back to Atlanta from Christmas in New York at the very tail end of 2000. One of the very first babies born in the new millenium, my younger daughter was about to turn one and my older daughter was five. It was getting harder for us to travel as a family, and I gazed out the back of our minivan at those iconic towers and wondered when I would ever see them again. The answer, of course, was never, as the terrorist attacks happened 9/11/01.

The Seals and Croft song titled "We May Never Pass this Way Again" came to me, and it would be a thought I carried throughout the journey. I was now heading to Pittsburgh by bus, for instance, and that's where my older daughter had attended college. We visited her many times there and absolutely loved that city. She had, in fact, taken this very bus to Pittsburgh from New York when we all met up for Christmas again while she was in college so many years after 9/11. Since she graduated, we had never been back there. I couldn't have imagined when we were there so often that *we may never pass this way again.* Going there today, even just to change buses, was a gift.

I remembered I still hadn't listened to the playlist she made for me. Right then would be the perfect time as we barreled across Pennsylvania. So I reclined my comfy seat, popped in my earbuds and watched the world go by as I listened to what she titled Momma's Adventure Playlist, featuring artists such as Florence and the Machine, The Wailin' Jenny's, Maggie Clifford, Rising Appalachia and more.

It was wonderful. I listened to that playlist every single day after that. The songs hit differently depending on where I was and what was happening. On that bus ride, the song "Desert Song" by a band named säje hit hardest: it talked about both reaching the desert and the ocean (which I interpreted as the Pacific, not the Atlantic where I had just been), and they both seemed impossibly far away to me right now. Yet, I could picture them, and I knew if I believed I could do it enough, I could manifest it. Besides, I was a New Yorker — *I do not quit.* If I said that enough to myself, I'd one day believe it, right?

I *had* quit something, and I always regretted it. In fact, it was my only regret in life. At the end of my junior year of high school at Maria Regina in Uniondale on Long Island, I was named the editor-in-chief of our newspaper. The then-graduating editor-in-chief and staff did a front-page above-the-fold article announcing this and featured a photo of me. It was intended to run the first week back in school.

Do you think I spent the summer learning how to be an editor-in-chief? Do you think I recruited a staff since the majority of the staff just graduated? Do you think I researched stories and developed an editorial calendar? Do you think I ever asked for help from my journalism teacher, who was the advisor for the newspaper? Do you think I even told my parents that I had been named the editor-in-chief and discussed with them what that might mean regarding my ability to keep my part-time job at the Waldbaum's supermarket, where (having switched from McDonald's) I was a cashier many nights after school and on weekends? You guessed it. A big fat no to all of it.

So the first day of school rolled around, and I had come up with only one possible solution to my problem. I had to quit. Seventeen-year-old me saw no other way forward. Did I quit graciously? Did I quit with a plan for how the paper could continue? Did I offer to help in the transition? No, no, no.

The first issue of the newspaper came out, written by who or how I do not know. The lead article had been rewritten to say the position was open and encouraged students to apply. But *they kept the picture*. They simply cut out my face and typed in the words "Your face here." I was clearly identifiable in the rest of the photo by my hair and what I was wearing. The entire school got this newspaper, and I sunk into my locker.

Mortified and increasingly tapped out from the school social scene, I stopped going to classes at least one day a week every single week that entire year (and still miraculously graduated 16th in my class). Instead, I drove down to the beach — yes, the Atlantic Ocean where I just dipped my bike tire — and I sat on a rock jetty and wrote bad poetry. And then I went to my job at Waldbaum's and talked with customers about the fresh vegetables they were buying and what they planned to do with them. Broccoli rabe!

Who knew? When my friends went off to great colleges, I stayed home and went to C.W. Post and rode horses. Poorly.

So, no, I did not want to quit again. I saw this journey, in part, as an opportunity to re-visit that regret and to make different choices this time. Quick aside: I did end up becoming the arts and entertainment editor of my college newspaper at Geneseo, and the reviews I wrote for that paper are what nabbed me my first corporate content creator job in New York City, so it's not quite the sob story I'm making it out to be. Things happen. Paths twist and turn. *"If you are at a fork in the road, take it,"* as the famous Yankee baseball player Yogi Berra said so eloquently. And if you feel, years later, that you took the wrong road, take another. It's okay.

Philly (hello again, old friend!), Harrisburg (great family of bike racks in front of the Rachel Carson Government Building!) and then Pittsburgh and its familiar yellow bridges welcomed me just as the sun set on the Allegheny, Ohio and Monongahela Rivers.

Dinner-time, I headed for the food options. Think of what you might have to choose from in an airport. Now, consider that my only and best choice for dinner here was from a pull-knob machine. I chose those crackers with the layer of that fake-cheese-peanut-butter stuff. They may have even been left over from the 1970s bike boom when Betty and my friend Janet rode their bikes on the Wantagh Parkway in support of building that new path, while I was riding my bike at that time all over Mineola.

That was dinner. Sure, I had snacks with me but there were only so many protein bars, nuts, chocolate chips, dates and oranges I could eat. Sometimes bus stations had some food choices nearby, but in general, it was not recommended that women leave the stations due to the relative risks of the surrounding neighborhoods.

Plus, I simply wasn't very mobile with all my stuff, despite how much I had pre-planned and streamlined. I hadn't realized that my fully-packed backpack, when on my back, pushed up my bike helmet from behind so that it was covering my eyes. My two-mile trip from Penn Station to my younger daughter's apartment in New York City made this abundantly clear, and there really wasn't a thing I could do about it besides get a different backpack.

I had gone to REI in Carle Place by our hotel to see if they had a pack more suited to using on a bike but came up short. I also realized that although the pack I had borrowed may be great for the Appalachian Trail, it didn't have enough compartments that were the right sizes for the kinds of things I brought with me for city and farm visits. I didn't know if what I needed existed. How could that be? I guess most people who crossed the country with a bike used panniers for all their stuff, which hung off the sides, front and back of their bikes, not on *their* backs, but I wasn't bike-touring so that did not serve my needs. Was I the first person to be crossing the country via bike, buses and trains and working on organic farms?

I boarded the bus to my next transfer at St. Louis, Missouri, and settled in for the evening. As night fell, I still had an empty seat next to me and was able to spread out for my overnight sleep. Janet's scarf wrapped around my head, my little snore-stopper on my nose and my headphones playing Celtic meditation music (which saved my sanity during that first tumultuous year of the pandemic), I dozed off just to have to reposition my legs every half hour or so. But it wasn't bad. I got some sleep.

Then, suddenly, the bus pulled into a station at around 1:00 AM and the bus driver put on the lights and told everyone there was a two-hour layover.

"Welcome to Indianapolis," he said.

I was not prepared for this.

It was like Zombie Land. Everyone was half asleep both on the bus and in the station. I knew I couldn't doze off as a woman alone, as some people had done on the benches. So I did the only thing I could in this circumstance. I made a TikTok!

The current trend was depicting a scene as if it were a Wes Anderson movie, so I worked my way around the station videotaping clips, with an emphasis on the typical traits of that director: symmetry, tableau compositions and specific color palettes.

I filmed the water fountain. My feet on the tile floor. The banana and muffin I purchased (worst muffin of the trip, by the way, but still a godsend after those crackers). I edited, added music and uploaded it all during this glorious gift of unexpected time in an Indiana bus station. It was fun, and fun mattered more than ever during these increasingly humorless times.

On bus number three, I couldn't fall back asleep. Just as with the other buses and trains, I gazed out the window and never tired of my sneak peeks into other worlds. My growing philosophy of radical non-judgment first adopted at Lish's goat farm led to me believing that every moment had a cultural anthropology and an art to it. This allowed me to find both meaning and beauty in everything I witnessed, and to try, somehow, to not take things personally.

In the past 10 years or so, I had learned to see my invisibility as an aging woman in America as a bit of an artistic superpower. I could explore without being questioned and had found this enabled me to shoot street photography, capturing many small and big moments in American life from public pianos to protests. I didn't have my good camera (which wasn't all that good) with me on this journey but I did enjoy life outside my bus and train windows through the new ways street photography had trained me to see.

As we approached St. Louis, I had a perfect view of the arch out the window right next to me on the other side of the bus, but the guy sitting there was sound asleep with his mouth wide open. I took the photo. It's a wonderful photo, but I may never share it because it might be embarrassing to him. This concern about other people's feelings does not make me the best photojournalist, and, in fact, stands in the way of me sharing some truths about this journey with you. I've had to make some hard moral decisions before being able to write this book. I wrestled with them even while writing my blog posts during the journey.

Here's where I landed: When this book is done, I want to be able to send a copy of it to every one of my hosts and thank them. I hope they will like how they are depicted after welcoming me into the privacy of their homes and, in many cases, sharing deeply personal stories with me. That may make the book less salacious, but I want you to stay with me here and trust that I am making the best decision. Assume I am leaving some things out, and that people's dignity matters more than me sharing every gory detail. Respect that I am respecting others. And help me do what I've set out to do here — simply shine a light on hope in this country.

These are the kinds of in-depth thoughts I had on the buses and trains, by the way. I never, ever got tired of the slow travel, you know. Never, not once. Not even during the final 72 hours of the journey across deserts, the border of Mexico, the Louisiana bayou and the Deep South. When I arrived back in Atlanta, I felt like Gene Wilder in the movie *Stir Crazy* when the guard opens the prison cell door to release him from solitary confinement and he says, "One more day. *Please.* Just one more day. I was just beginning to get into myself."

Does that mean I am a die-hard introvert who enjoyed being "alone together" with strangers? Does that mean I am a woman who has spent a lifetime on other people's schedules (school, work, society) and needed to hear the beat of my own heart for a while? Does that mean I am an exhausted American who wanted to reconnect with what makes this country special? Maybe all of that. Maybe that's you, too. Or maybe you're just here for the ride, curious to find out what happened next.

So we arrived in Joplin, Missouri, or rather six miles/10 kilometers on its outskirts at a Phillips 66 gas station located right in the middle of empty fields as far as you could see. The bus stop was moved from Downtown Joplin in 2015 so it would be closer to Interstate 44, which in some parts replaced Route 66 and in some parts aligned with its historic remains.

Called The Mother Road and traversing from Chicago to Santa Monica, Route 66 transformed America by both increasing access to the country and glamorizing car culture. Its replacement by highways devastated small towns that relied on people passing through, who now had a faster route.

Some of these towns became actual ghost towns. I would, in fact, be staying spitting distance from Route 66 and just a mile or so from the ghost town of Avilla, Missouri, where 125 souls are still believed to exist. There were old broken-down buildings, colorful murals and an actual working US Post Office, all of which I looked forward to visiting on my bike and photographing.

Right then, however, I was sitting on a curb waiting for Candida. I was so hungry I can't even put it in words, and I had to use the bathroom. When I tried to walk my small folding bike into the gas station, the clerk adamantly told me to leave, that no bikes were allowed inside. The clerk was busy with the constant stream of truckers coming in and I didn't feel comfortable leaving my stuff or asking anyone to watch it so I just sucked it up (literally) and sat there.

I had texted Candida to let her know I'd be in around 1:00 PM. When no one was there to meet me, I left a message on her home phone machine and I messaged her WWOOF profile, thinking perhaps she hadn't gotten my text. By 2:25 PM, I re-texted her.

"I'm trying to confirm someone is coming?" I asked.

I had some trauma when I was a child (haven't we all?) and the thing that triggers it most is when I feel like I've been forgotten. It could be as simple as waiting a long time for a take-out order or a coffee. It certainly could be sitting on a curb in a gas station in the middle of nowhere waiting for someone I don't know to pick me up. I felt vulnerable, exposed and, yes, scared. *What was I doing?* What was a grown woman, a seasoned professional, a homeowner, a mom, doing sitting on this curb like yesterday's garbage?

Candida arrived and I immediately liked her. She had had some challenges of her own, *big* challenges, and I could sympathize with that. In fact, she shared that she considered cancelling my workstay because of what she was juggling but she didn't want to do that to me.

There. Then. That's when we both should have just thrown in the towel. But hindsight is 20/20, right? And we were both clearly trying. Besides, I had no other options for *the next five weeks*.

I then asked her about the brace on her arm. She told me she had had a driving incident and her doctor thinks she has narcolepsy. She told me this as we were barreling down a highway. Was she kidding? Did that matter? Have I mentioned how nervous I am in cars? This would not be the only time I wanted to jump out of a car on this journey.

We passed Avilla and I wanted to stop and see it so badly but knew I'd have plenty of time to ride my bike there once I settled in. Then, we stopped at the home of a friend of hers to drop off fresh eggs. I thought it was going to be a very quick stop, but we ended up sitting at the kitchen table for a long while, me eyeing the bread or cake or whatever that delectable was on the counter the whole time and trying to squelch the growling in my stomach. We would be at the sanctuary shortly. All would be well.

Candida and her friend talked in depth about the long horseback ride they were going to take that Saturday, and it was clear that she intended for me to participate in that. Some of their comments led me to think that they made assumptions because I had said I had some riding experience and I was from Long Island, which has a very strong presence on the "riding circuit." Some of her horses are retired race horses. Some are rescues and are what's considered "green," which means they need a lot more training to be comfortably rideable. None of them are Rooster. No part of me intended to ride way over my head on 10,000 acres/4,000 hectares of open land. I could already see the obituary — and it wasn't the aspirational one I had imagined!

What's more, I discovered that Candida worked off-farm Monday through Friday, but not nearby like Lish did in Hurdle Mills. *Six hours away* in Illinois! This was what I considered to be an important piece of information that I had never been told. The final red flag was yet to come.

We arrived at Candida's home and horse sanctuary and at this point I just wanted to ground myself. Settle in. Unpack. Tour the place. Get a feel for what was expected of me. Go to the bathroom. *Eat.*

And then I saw the camper where I would be staying.

It was disgusting. The door was flung open. The bedroom had dirty sheets and blankets just piled on it. The water didn't work. And there were rodent droppings *everywhere*. The floor. The counters. The bathroom.

*I could clean this,* I thought to myself. I had fixed up The Tin Can at Lish's. I could put flowers in a jar. It would be cute. It would be okay. There'd be *TikToks*.

But then I opened the utensil draw, and as they say, that was the straw that broke the camel's back (although I wouldn't get to camels for a couple of months yet). It was so filled with rodent droppings — all over every single fork, spoon and knife — that I took a photo of it to send to my husband, which I didn't send until later that evening because I needed to figure this all out first.

These accommodations clearly did not meet WWOOF standards, and they were a health hazard. I took a deep breath and came outside to talk with Candida. I asked her about food, of which there was currently none although she said we could drive to get some tonight (my life flashed as I thought of more car rides and narcolepsy).

I then asked about the daily tasks, especially with her not even going to be there all week. I wasn't all that comfortable with either answer, and I shared that my initial reaction to the situation was "a lot" and I needed a few minutes to process my thoughts. Maybe we should have just agreed it wasn't a good fit — I suppose she was not that high on me right then either.

She said she was going to the house to get clean sheets and blankets, and I went inside the camper again. *Could I make this work?* I asked myself as objectively as I could. *Radical non-judgment, radical non-judgment,* I told myself. And if I couldn't, what exactly would I do instead for the next five weeks? Was this the end of the journey? My eyes filled with tears. No. No, I could not quit.

I stood there a moment and prayed. I had left Catholicism behind at Maria Regina High School but had enjoyed a direct line to my Higher Power ever since. My daily prayer went like this:

*Thank you for the beauty and glory and honor of this day. May I hear and heed your calling for me for today.*

Standing in that camper, I added this plea for guidance: *Help me to bravely and confidently trust your journey for me, God.* I knew that God worked through others and that the world would conspire in support of me and my purpose here on Earth, whatever that ends up being, if I could just *not quit* before the miracle (as my mother always recommends).

I then imagined night falling, which would not be that long from now, and the nocturnal life that clearly thrived right there where I would be sleeping. No amount of last-minute cleaning was going to change that. I would have rodents running over my body. There was no debate about that.

If there was one thing I could say about The Tin Can at Lish's farm, there were no rodents inside it. In fact, I had researched it while I was there, wondering why no WWOOFers had left a review mentioning the rest of its questionable condition, and I discovered that a couple had actually spent their time at Spinning Plates Farm improving that trailer extensively. After reading about their labors of love, I felt enveloped in it and grateful for its new floor and protection from rain and rodents. Could I feel that way here, too?

I opened the utensil drawer again, and recoiled yet again. I was a long way from Rats, the rat-free restaurant where Mindy took me.

No.

No, I could not stay here.

The universe was sending me a message and, however much I tried to deny it, it was loud, clear and simple.

Quit.

No, don't quit the journey. Not yet. Just quit *here*.

But what would I do next?

I had a reservation at a budget hotel in Joplin for five weeks from now. I originally intended to spend a night there before heading to Denver and Boulder because that's the motel chain where my family used to stay on our road trips and I wanted to do a story about Route 66 and the heyday of car travel. I was also curious what memories would be tickled alive and how the motel — and I —had changed over the years.

On my one singular day in Joplin, I planned to visit the location of the most deadly tornado in US history during the week of its 12th anniversary. I wanted to do a story about climate-related improvements the city may have made since then. I knew they got a lot of advice from a conservative small town in Kansas named Greensburg that had been destroyed by a tornado as well, and had built back using eco-friendly principles, as I had written a story years ago for a national magazine about that city — which I even considered visiting on this journey, but the bus didn't go there.

So I called the hotel.

"Hello?" The desk clerk answered, indicating they were now part of a larger family of hotels.

"Yes, I have a reservation in five weeks. I was wondering if I could change it?"

She looked it up and then asked, "When would you like to change it for?"

I paused a moment at the crossroads of this decision and thought of Yogi Berra. *When you get to a fork in the road, take it. Especially if it's covered in rodent droppings.*

"Now," I replied. "How does *now* sound?"

She paused a moment and then answered enthusiastically, "We happen to have an opening!"

I booked a room for two nights, one of which was not in my budget. I knew that if I started blowing my budget much more, the journey would have to end. We didn't have fat in our finances for me to be traipsing around the country wasting money. The whole charm of this journey was that it was going to cost less than if I stayed home at the bottom of the hill in suburbia. My times at farms could include a lot of what I called "zero spend days" (and had already in North Carolina) so that there was a little more money in the budget for the cities. But now I was looking at five weeks of *no farm*. Things were not looking good. And I still had to tell Candida.

This was, no doubt, one of the worst moments of my trip (and, oh yes, there were more). There is a very strong chance that I did not handle it gracefully and that I am in fact the asshole (as that AITA — Am I the Asshole? — trend on social media asks).

I tried. I tried as hard as I could. I am sorry, Candida, that it did not work out. I can't put in words how much I was looking forward to those five weeks. No ghost town and no Memorial Day parade for me. No grant application for you. As my mother has been reciting for years now, *God grant me the serenity to accept the things I cannot change, the courage to change the things I can, and the wisdom to know the difference.* I felt neither serene, courageous nor wise.

Later that night in Room 112 at the modest hotel in Joplin, Missouri, I wrote my review on WWOOF. Both WWOOFers and the WWOOF hosts can leave reviews. Like with the rideshare companies, you don't get to see what the host wrote until you post your own. I shared that it didn't work out for me but would surely be a better fit for someone else. For instance, some WWOOFers travel with their own RVs — that would have worked out well there. I wish I never saw what Candida wrote about me. In addition to other things, she was particularly angry that she picked me up at the gas station and then drove me the 28 miles/45 kilometers back to my hotel where the cheap hotels were located (I had offered to take a rideshare) and I had thus wasted her day.

The forecast predicted pouring rain the next day. That would typically be no problem — I had rain gear with me, and I had just spent weeks at Lish's farm very happily in the rain. Besides, I had a long history of riding my bike in all kinds of weather. But this was tornado country, and that got my attention. A tornado had hit my Metro Atlanta city when my older daughter was three and I still, to this day, huddle in the half-bathroom with my bike helmet on whenever there is a tornado warning.

I was hoping I would be able to go ahead with my stories about Joplin, despite everything. But first, I had to figure out what I was going to do about this big fat hole in my schedule now. If I haven't made it quite clear to you yet, *I did not want to quit.* But what were my options?

Hubby and I were, of course, texting back and forth. No matter what I said, he was supportive. No "You should do this, " or "This is crazy; you need to come home" or even "There is no shame in stopping." He knew how much this meant to me, and he had my back. I already knew that from our 33-year marriage, of course, but it still blew me away. He truly believed in me, and I needed to believe in myself.

I knew I had options; I just didn't know what they were yet. I knew that even as I sat there eating a Greek salad (finally!) from the gas station next door to the hotel, God had my back, too. But how?

"You're smarter than the average bear," I told myself, as I often had in jest over the years, using a line from the classic cartoon from my childhood, Yogi Bear (not to be confused with Yogi Berra, but, yes, actually inspired by him).

"Think, think, think," I ordered myself, quoting Winnie the Pooh.

What bear had I left out? Oh, Smokey the Bear. It would be a little while yet on the journey before I thought of that forest-fire-fighter.

There was one idea my husband and I had discussed that warranted consideration. He, our younger daughter and I were all convening in Los Angeles near the end of my journey for my 60th birthday and our older daughter's bridal shower, so I wanted to stick with the timeframe I had laid out because it got me into LA just in time for that. But, truth be told, I *could* go home — not to quit; just to pause for the five weeks I would have spent at the horse sanctuary, and I could then hop on a series of train connections from Atlanta to Denver and be back on schedule with Elise's homestead near Denver in Boulder.

That was a thought. Do laundry. Eat. Sleep in my own bed. Spend some unexpected time with my husband and my mother. Whack back the garden a bit more. But I felt that the chances of getting de-railed were too high.

I suddenly remembered Christi. Christi was the office manager at Heartland Farm, the alpaca ranch and eco-spirituality center five hours away in Kansas. After I had cancelled with them due to the bus stop suspension, she had messaged me to let me know that she would be passing through Joplin in early May if I wanted to drive back with her at that point. I had thanked her but told her I had already committed to the five weeks with Candida and couldn't leave early.

But here we now were! It was a week shy of the date she mentioned, so I would have to figure out what I would do in the meantime (did the hotel have an opening for a desk clerk?), but maybe this was the answer!

I also texted Elise, my upcoming WWOOF host in Boulder. Maybe I could push on to Boulder early and stay there two months (the three planned weeks plus this suddenly-available five weeks). That wasn't out of the question for a WWOOF length-of-stay, although a bit risky since I didn't know how I would like it there yet but the photos online of the room for WWOOFers was beautiful. Plus, Boulder was one of the most bike-friendly cities in the United States and that was sure to be a joy. This was an option!

Christi wrote back that she was no longer going to Joplin. Elise wrote that she was out of town and would be for another week but that this was a possibility. She suggested I contact a friend of hers named Farmer Earth to see if I could go to his farm for the week before her return. I sent a message to Farmer Earth and called it a night.

The next morning, I got a message from Farmer Earth. He wanted to have a video chat, which we did. He had other WWOOFers already but could offer me a tent to stay in while I would be there. I was grateful for the offer and was considering it, but I couldn't help feeling farther and farther away from the charming tiny home I had stayed in at the farm in Mableton, Georgia where I pilot-tested this journey. Would everywhere I go be unready for me or really, really roughing it?

I was willing to provide free labor for 20-30 hours a week. The barter deal is you get acceptable accommodations and three healthy meals a day in return. Why was I starting to feel like the chickens were living better at these places? WWOOF social media sites were filled with inviting accommodations. Or was that only in Europe? Was this subpar treatment of WWOOFers only in the United States, I wondered? And if so, how did that bode for the rest of my journey?

*Maybe I should just go home,* I pondered. *Just get off your high horse. Maybe this isn't for me. Candida said if I couldn't handle a little mouse, how would I do with a snake? I've already WWOOFed at two farms. Maybe that's enough.*

That's what my sweatshirt said, right? *You are enough.*

And then, when I had almost resigned myself to being at the end of the line, I got a call from Christi.

# 4

## Heaven on Earth

"We're coming to get you," Christi said, excited.

"You're coming to get me?" I gasped. "That's 10 hours round-trip!"

"I asked Sister Jane and she said yes. Tre and I are coming to get you." Tre was the social media manager.

Wait. What? These people whom I knew for all of an hour on a Zoom call — correction, I had actually never met Tre yet — deemed me worth enough to drive 10 hours to get? My brain nearly exploded trying to comprehend this. Christi never asked a question about what happened at my planned Missouri workstay. *She didn't care.*

"We're coming," she said again, adamantly.

Even as I write this months later, I'm choked up remembering how it felt in that modest hotel room in that rainy Midwestern city to hear a veritable stranger say those words to me, especially after what just happened, after I had "wasted" Candida's day following my 30-hour bus ride to her farm.

I remember thinking *this is God's work*. And suddenly, there were no more questions. No more doubts. No more options. I belonged in Kansas. Of this, I was entirely, unequivocally certain. I heard — and heeded — God's calling for me.

A quick tap tap tap on my phone and I saw I could get a bus from Joplin to Wichita, Kansas the next day so that Christi and Tre would only need to drive four hours round-trip instead of 10. As if *that* were a short distance!

My route required me to change buses in Oklahoma City. The next morning, engulfed in fog, my bus ran two hours late, which resulted in my missing my connection in Oklahoma. Which meant another un-budgeted hotel night, this time at a different hotel chain walking distance from the bus station, in the rain, past two far seedier-looking motels.

I didn't get upset or anxious about it. I knew I was exactly where I was meant to be today, tomorrow, forever. I was finally learning to truly trust the journey. I even swam in the hotel's indoor pool, in the dark, alone. And it was glorious. I had brought my bathing suit with me for one reason only — my final farm, in the High Desert of California, had an outdoor pool. I hadn't expected the gift of this night's swim. While backstroking from one end to the other, I realized the ability to swim, as well as ride a bicycle, is potentially life-saving more now than ever with our growing climate disasters and I felt grateful to still be able to do both.

Luckily, Christi and Tre hadn't left Kansas yet when I had realized I would probably not make it to Wichita that day. Since the next day was a Saturday, I asked Christi if we should plan on Monday to connect. What's a few more hotel nights, right?

Christi replied, "No, no, no. We'll come Saturday. The annual alpaca shearing is Sunday morning, and you're not gonna want to miss that! It's no problem at all, although we can't leave here until Open Farm Day ends so we won't get in to Wichita until early evening."

"Are you sure?" I asked. That seemed like a very long day for them.

Christi did not miss a beat. " We're looking forward to it — and you," she replied.

If you are still doubting whether there's hope in America anymore. Or beauty. Or love. Or goodness. I'd like to introduce you to Christi, Tre, Sister Jane and everyone else at Heartland Farm in Pawnee Rock, Kansas. Because of them, my life was about to change forever.

My younger daughter called while I was writing this part of the book and I told her how I originally thought I would just publish my collective blog posts from this journey, and had even compiled them in a 50,000-word draft. But when I realized that the posts fell flat, I started completely over, right down to the blank first page. She asked why and I replied, "When I wrote the blog posts, I couldn't see the big picture yet and how all the pieces added up. For instance, I didn't know when I was blogging about that saga in Missouri that Kansas was about to happen."

She said, "That line is a metaphor. Kansas about to happen is the good about to come in life, no matter where."

*Don't quit before the miracle.*

We turned off the dirt road onto a quarter-mile gravel driveway in the stillness of the night, Christi's car filled with my bike and other travel stuff, along with my groceries from the Walmart in Wichita and our nonstop laughter along the drive. I had gotten the opportunity to explore Wichita on my bike for a few hours before they arrived, my helmet pushed partly over my eyes by my backpack, and, with this fleeting rubber-hits-the-road knowledge, it was nice to hear about their experiences in and around Wichita, Great Bend, and elsewhere. Christi and her husband raised Scottish Highland cows. Tre helped care for her mother. Again, it hit me how many ways there are to live a life.

When I had gotten off the bus in Wichita, by the way, a woman and her adult son came over to me to comment as I was snapping open my bike. We got to talking, as usually happens, and I asked if they had hope, of course. The son said a quick, "No."

I thought I'd suggest something small and said that windmills I had passed on a prior bus had given me hope. He then told me lots of details about windmills, which was interesting. His mother stepped back and let us talk, seeming to enjoy it.

They then hugged quickly, he left to catch his bus, and I asked her if she felt hope. Her eyes moist, she replied, "Today I do. He's on his way to rehab."

We just stood there, both mothers, both in tears, and then hugged. I once again felt like I was exactly where I was supposed to be, connecting with humanity.

Later at the supermarket, Christi gave me my weekly stipend of $40, which went quickly. Plus, I bought an additional $95 worth of food supplies — olive oil, salt, pepper, beans, rice, chickpea pasta, hummus, tofu, veggies, fruits, crackers, and my luxury snack throughout the journey, dark chocolate chips. *You are enough*, my sweatshirt said to myself and everyone else. You *have* enough, I additionally told myself but I also knew I needed a certain amount of actual food, quantitatively, to sustain my healthy diet and daily level of physical activity. Knowing how much to buy was a gamble.

There would be group lunches a few days a week, but I would be cooking for myself the rest of the time. I wasn't sure what was available on the farm yet for my use, and I didn't know when I would get to a supermarket again — and, if you want to know the truth, I was hungry in a way that took, really, two months to satiate. Maybe it wasn't just physical. So I bought what I anticipated

I'd need, knowing many of the items would be one-time purchases that would last the length of my stay so it would even out.

It was after 11:00 PM by this time and Christi drove slowly so as not to wake the Sisters, who lived in the large white main farmhouse. She pointed to a smaller white clapboard house, silhouetted in the dark, and said, "That's Elm House. That's *your* house."

My house. *My house.*

And then it kept getting better.

They did a quick driving tour on the circular driveway, lit by moon and stars. They pointed out the alpaca barn. The spinning/pottery studio. The silo with rainbow windows converted into a meditation space. The chicken barn. The office. The gift shop that sells soft, warm alpaca-wool socks and freshly-made jams.

When they opened the door to my spotlessly-cleaned, fully equipped house, my eyes immediately fixated on the kitchen island where there sat a loaf of freshly baked bread. For *me*. Next to it was an unopened jar of sand plum jam, made from native plums picked from wild trees on the side of the dirt road by an 85-year old sister named Sister Imelda, who was one of the founders of this Heaven-on-Earth in the 1970s, back when Betty and Janet were riding bikes on the Wantagh Parkway and I was riding on the Meadowbrook.

Christi and Tre helped me unpack and left me to make myself at home. They told me I would meet Terra, the farm manager, the next morning at 8:00 AM to get a tour of the farm prior to the alpaca shearing, in which I'd get to participate.

I walked slowly from spotlessly-clean room to room. Full kitchen. Three bedrooms. Wood floor. Beautiful handmade quilts on every bed and hanging on the living room wall. Indoor modern bathroom (hurray). Washing machine. Wooden blinds. Ceiling fans. Fresh eggs in the fridge and fruit in a bowl. I thought of how I almost disrespected myself enough to accept a filthy, rodent-infested old camper elsewhere. Thank God, and these self-less souls in Kansas, that I didn't. I snapped photos of the quilts and texted them to my mother. She was a quilter — and an ex-nun, by the way. So this all hit home.

Hungry and tired, I sliced the bread, warmed it and slathered it with butter and jam. I sat in the tub as the water filled (my first of two baths on the entire journey) and ate it, butter running down my chin.

I remembered the very first time I ever baked bread, in my college apartment in Geneseo with my roommate Kristin. We didn't realize how long it would take, between all the rising and waiting, and were both in bed when it was finally ready. We sat there in the dark, in our beds, and ate the fresh-from-the-oven warm bread, butter running down our chins. For almost 40 years now, we often said mid-conversation miles away from each other, "Remember the bread?"

I will remember this bread forever, too.

The next song on my Momma's Adventure Playlist included one line over and over again. *There will be better days. There will be better days. There will be better days.*

*No. No, there would not,* I thought to myself. *It could not get any better than this.*

And then it did.

The first light of morning streamed through the stained glass window on the front door. Drawn to it like moths to fire, I opened the door and stood there awe-stricken on the porch. The sun was rising directly in front of me, the endless expanse of land and sky called Kansas stretching out in every direction. It occurred to me, incredulously, that this would be my every morning here! Awe has two sides, and I had gone from awful to awesome overnight.

I ran barefoot outside between two trees and did my little dance. Lingering with the cool grass between my toes, I then practiced my yoga, as I had in the repurposed tobacco fields of North Carolina. I would go on to do my vinyasa flow overlooking a valley in Colorado, in the llama's favorite patch of sagebrush as well as in the Hare Krishna temple in Utah, in an abandoned gold mine in California, and even on the rail system's panoramic train car, balancing precariously, deep in the heart of Texas.

I worshiped nature, and this full-bodied presence was my prayer every morning. In fact, except for the brief, heartfelt and often funny prayers offered by the Sisters before lunches, my own personal prayers, spoken conversationally to my Higher Power in an ongoing dialogue throughout the day, would be the only prayer I encountered while here. Any concern I might have had (which I really didn't) of being judged for leaving Catholicism or feeling pressure to participate in rituals that are not part of my practice were unfounded.

I was, of course, open to both the cultural anthropology and the art of different faith-based practices. That would benefit me when visiting the Sisters' interesting Mother House in Great Bend, Kansas 14 miles/23 kilometers away to drop off eggs; at the astounding Hare Krishna temple's weekly Love Feasts and at Cowboy Church (yep; it's a thing), both in Utah; and at a 200-student Shabbat dinner on a college campus in southern California.

Christi had given me enough weekly timesheets to cover my stay, a printout of the typical daily schedule, and a page of photos of every one of the 17 alpacas with their names. We were a long way from North Carolina's paper plate on the refrigerator!

Jasper. Joy. Quivira. I was excited to meet them. I walked past the extensive clotheslines — bras, panties and farm clothes already swinging from them — and entered the large barn. Terra was already scooping alpaca poop and I happily joined her. In the hierarchy of poop and its yuck factor, alpaca poop was very low. Pelleted like rabbit manure, it wasn't messy, didn't smell, and was easy to scoop. Rabbit, goat, alpaca and llama manure can be used directly on gardens, by the way, without composting it first, so it was particularly valuable here on the farm as there were two very large uncovered gardens. There was also what's called a high tunnel, which is typically a large structure made from steel and covered with polyethylene that extends the growing season by providing protection for crops.

My schedule included lots of animal chores — Terra was training me to care for both the alpacas and the chickens — and about two hours of garden work each day. Fresh off my chicken care at both Spinning Plates farm in North Carolina and Our Giving Garden in Mableton back in Georgia, I was excited for that. The alpacas would be new, and what was not to love about them?

Alpacas are part of the camelid family. This includes camels, llamas, alpacas and their wild relatives guanacos (most similar to llamas) and vicuñas (most similar to alpacas). Alpacas are pretty much the weight of adult humans (although more than my weight), about 120-180 pounds/54-82 kilograms, and are thus about half the size of llamas. Like llamas, they have three stomachs and are herbivores, but they have different faces, back slopes and ear shapes than llamas. They all, of course, have stunningly beautiful eye lashes. Alpacas are prized on farms for their valuable fleece. Both are used for manure and breeding, and llamas can also be used as guard animals.

Aren't *I* fun at a party? But wait, there's more.

Llamas are also used as pack animals for trekking, and I would get a chance to help train some just a bit at the Hare Krishna temple in Utah later on my journey. And yes, I know what question you are thinking. It's the first and often only one folks ask when I mention I worked with both types of these herds. *Do they really spit?* As Vai at the Hare Krishna temple says, "Spit happens."

Spitting is indeed a complex form of communication for both alpacas and llamas, and there are three stages of spitting. You do not want to be on the receiving end of stage three and will probably be relieved to know they mostly spit at each other — although I felt like I was dodging it constantly at my fourth and final herd in the High Desert of California!

The alpaca shearing in Kansas was the only camelid shearing in which I got to participate, and I lived to tell about it! As Terra, Sister Jane and another Sister named Rene wrangled alpacas by cornering them and bear-hugging their necks, a former Sister and dear friend of Sister Jane's named Lila and I wrestled them into harnesses and attached leads. We then walked them out a few at a time to the large pavilion where the shearing was taking place.

A professional shearer and his partner had flown in from Minnesota for the gig, which included not just our alpacas but also alpacas and llamas from others in the community who were invited to join in on the group rate.

The professionals sheared each alpaca in just three minutes, and a team of us worked swiftly to gather the subsequent fleece with large scoop-like tools. We stuffed it into plastic bags, saved and reused from year to year and marked with each alpaca's name since the yarn was packaged and marked accordingly so craftspeople and artisans could be sure they were getting a consistent color by buying the yarn from the same animal. This was sold in the farm's gift shop for 30-something dollars a skein — valuable stuff.

Just as with spitting, there were three classifications of fleece. "Firsts," the best quality, were the main blanket of fleece off the alpacas' backs. This was used for yarn and roving, which was fiber that has been processed but not yet spun into yarn and can be used for other textile arts. "Seconds" were the fleece off of the neck, which was used for things like warm, moisture-wicking, naturally-antimicrobial shoe inserts, which were sold in the farm's gift shop as well. "Thirds" were the fleece from the legs and bellies and could be used for felting or pillow stuffing — although Terra had another idea.

Rocking color-coordinated work clothes from Duluth Trading Company each day, Terra was a pink-hair-streaked, pierced ray of Millennial sunshine. She had majored in Environmental Science and did a research-based internship at the famous Biosphere in

Tucson, Arizona, which taught her much but also made it clear to her that she wanted to be on the farm, not in the laboratory.

As native to Kansas as the dried sunflowers in the field surrounding the high tunnel vegetable garden, she knew the land and the impacts of this multiyear drought. She rotated the alpacas on the range land to provide enough forage for the herd, but it was a concern. It wasn't growing fast enough and her rain gauge had recorded only eight-tenths of an inch of rain as the biggest downpour in the last year and a half.

She knew there may be a day not long off when there simply won't be enough grass growing to graze on. Supplemental brome hay had filled the void so far but it was expensive to buy and she wished they could grow it themselves on the farm, as they used to.

In the gardens, she was experimenting with alpaca fleece as a sustainable weed cover in the aisles, layered "lasagna-style" between empty paper feed bags and the woody remains of the brome after the alpacas ate the green stuff. It would also help preserve rainwater, if it ever came, by directing it to rows where seeds, soon to be planted, would be thirsty.

I loved the idea and was excited that I got to help her do this, using the fleece called "thirds." As we worked, we talked. We shared deep dark stories from our lives. And we shared hope. Woman to woman. Generation to generation.

After a week of side-by-side training, I was pretty much on my own feeding the alpacas in the morning and at night, walking the girls out to the range and then later the boys, cleaning the barn and barnyard, and, on Lila's days off, feeding the chickens, and gathering and washing the eggs. I'd end each day putting the chickens to bed. I would often cross paths with Terra in the gardens and hoop house and we would work on something together. It was a lovely flow and I enjoyed the mix of independent and collaborative work.

I had volunteered to put the chickens to bed while I was there, even on my one day off each week, because when I asked what chore everyone hated most, that's the one they identified. It wasn't because it was a bad chore — in fact, it was easy and just took a few moments if you waited long enough, because the chickens groom and put themselves to bed right as the sun set. You really just need to lock up the coop to protect the chickens from predators, such as the raccoons that stood on the edge of the chicken run and watched me each night. The thing folks hated was how late it was when the sun would set in May. They were done, finished, *jammied*, and didn't want to have to go out there again.

I loved it. I would make myself dinner, often using fresh greens and herbs from the gardens, and do some writing. Next, I would ride my bike around the paths in the woods and meadows and watch the sunset over the hoop house and hay bales. I'd then make a video call to my mother in her independent living facility half a country away in Alpharetta, Georgia and she and I would watch as the chickens marched into their large coop, perched themselves in the rafters and cooed gently. I'd then take my mom to see the alpacas as they snuggled up on the ground on their folded legs in their barn.

These precious moments were undoubtedly some of the best times she and I have ever spent together, and I consider them a priceless gift from this journey. My mother and I both laughed when we remembered people worried about me leaving her.

My daily bike ride around the block here covered six miles/10 kilometers, passing large commercial farms and often not one car, truck or human. There were cows at the first and second turns but after that, nothing but dirt road, yet another type of swaying golden grasses (you know how I love them), wildflowers, telephone poles that reminded me of church crosses, endless sky and the constant avian activity of the Central Flyway migratory bird route. Keep New York's bridges, plus Boulder's bike park and LA's ocean path yet-to-come. Give me Kansas forever and I think I'd be happy. *There are so many ways to live a life.*

This thought was not hard to keep front and center as I rode right in the center of the roads, singing my heart out. Usually it was songs from Momma's Adventure Playlist — a favorite lyric being *Earth my body; Water my blood; Air my breathe and Fire my spirit* — but one day it was the latest TikTok trend, Adam Lambert's rendition, as Cher, of the song "The Muffin Man."

I was having fun here in Kansas, both on and off the farm, and I knew fun mattered more than ever. In fact, I believe centering joy is an act of resistance as the world turns and burns out of control. It engages all the senses and provides the mental and physical fortitude to help us make sense of — or escape temporarily — the insanity that surrounds us.

It does not help, however, when a tornado rolls is, and that was happening right in front of me. *And I got a flat.*

"Oh shit, oh shit, oh shit," I said out loud to the chattering birds as they noisily alerted each other and dove for cover. Scenes from memoirs I had read of people bike-touring across the USA flashed though my mind.

*Jump in the ditch*, I told myself, looking out at this flat-as-a-pancake landscape. *If it gets closer, jump in the ditch. Cover yourself with the bike. Lay low.*

The dark clouds were increasingly swirling and getting closer. I was still halfway away from the farm, and that meant I needed to ride into the looming disaster just a little longer before I could turn the corner away from it. I tried to do high-level calculations of a speed-of-movement comparison between the clouds and my bike, but may I remind you I spent my senior year of high school writing bad poetry on a rock jetty instead of in college-level math classes?

"Holy mother of God, I'm going to die in a tornado in Kansas!" I screamed, every childhood fear from the classic movie *The Wizard of Oz* coming to life right in front of me. Cue the Wicked Witch on the bike! Cue the Flying Monkeys! I thought of all those nights coiled up in my half-bathroom in Metro Atlanta with my girls, and then later after they left home, with my bike helmet on. And here I was, with my bike helmet on, riding ferociously on a small folding bike with a flat tire into the wind to my possible death.

*Trust the journey. Trust the journey. Trust the journey,* I prayed over and over again.

As I turned the next corner, facing the growing certainty of a calamity, I stopped riding and contacted Terra. "I'm in trouble. Can you come get me?" I texted. I hated to drag her out and put her in danger as well, but my expert calculations as a poet indicated that there was still time for her to get me in the truck, and probably not time for me to get home on the bike. She told me she was leaving immediately.

And then I faced a dilemma.

A truck raced up alongside me and stopped. A worried man inside rolled down his window and said, "You shouldn't be out here. That storm is huge. There's a tornado warning over in Larned. And it's heading our way."

I didn't know where Larned was, but I knew I was in danger. I thanked him, and then we both just looked at each silently a moment. The unspoken words were, "Do you want to get in a truck with a strange man and save your life?" It might be a few minutes yet before Terra reached me. Those few minutes might make all the difference.

But then I will have put *her* in danger for no reason. And if I waited for her and we got caught in the tornado, at least we could try to help each other. But this was a gamble.

What would you have done?

"I . . . called for help already," I finally replied. "She'll be here very soon. I'm okay."

He lingered a moment longer, just looking at me, thinking perhaps what a fool I was. My heart broke when I saw him reverse the truck and speed backwards on the dirt road to the nearest farm I had passed. He must have been looking out the window at the storm or sitting on the porch way back from the road when I passed. He must have debated with himself what to do, and then jumped in the truck and sped up to save me. He maybe had his own daughters and knew I had been trained not to get in a vehicle with a man I don't know. He must have appreciated how hard that decision was under the circumstances.

I kept trudging along in the headwinds on my broken bike and finally turned the corner away from the storm, but it was closing in on me quickly. Too quickly. And then, out of seemingly nowhere, I saw a plume of dirt kicking up on the road and Terra's truck appeared. I flung my bike into it and hopped into the passenger seat as she swung the truck around in the unpaved intersection of Avenue X and County Road 390 and tore for home.

The storm battered the drought-stricken farm all night. But the tornado spared us. I was understandably nervous whenever I rode my bike after that. I always made sure to check the weather, let folks know I was out on my bike in case I needed to be rescued again, and not travel too far from the farm, although the six-mile around-the-block journey was the shortest I could really do.

I had a spare bike tire tube with me and enjoyed changing it in the farm workshop, which had a full supply of tools well beyond the awkward multitool I carried with me. This was clutch because I hadn't realized my wheels did not have quick releases on them, so I needed a wrench to remove the nut and bolt from the tire with the flat in order to fix it, and I didn't have a wrench with me.

I would end up having a total of six flats on this journey — two in Kansas, two in Colorado and two in Utah. I ordered a replacement tube online each time I got a flat (or picked it up at a bike shop when I got to Boulder and Utah) so I always had a spare. I bought a wrench in Boulder, too. I carried my bike supplies, including a hand pump, in a little bag that attached quickly via Velcro to my handlebars,

I decided to change the flats instead of patch them because I wanted to be entirely sure they were working properly, plus I saved them to make more BikeBloom earrings. I thought it might be fun to have a collection specifically from this journey.

If you want to know the truth, I didn't actually believe the *bike* would make it through the trip. Before I left home, I had braced myself for the possibility that it would break or get stolen or need to be abandoned by me at some point because it wouldn't be allowed on some local bus or train that was critical to my safety or forward movement.

My husband had even suggested not bringing the bike and asked if I could rent one or use bikeshare throughout the journey instead. I told him that in addition to general transportation and mental-health joy, I needed it for three safety reasons: as a getaway vehicle, as a barrier and as a weapon. This didn't mean my trips were dangerous. This meant leaving my house as a woman was dangerous, and I had a much bigger survival tool box than my little multitool to address that.

This also meant that every single bike ride was precious, and I was acutely aware of that. As always, I reminded myself there would be a day I could no longer ride this bike, and there would also be a day I couldn't no longer ride *any* bike. Those days had not yet come.

It rained again. A gully gusher. A toad strangler. Rare here, and desperately needed — a little more than three inches, plus the inch the week before and another little drizzle. One night, the glass door shattered leading to the apartment in the basement of my house, where Lila lived and where there was a separate commercial kitchen where Sister Imelda baked bread and made jam— and which served as my evacuation destination, if needed, per Sister Jane. In total, we had a solid third of the expected annual rainfall in the three weeks since I'd arrived, and the ponds and creek and moods showed a positive ripple effect.

Corn was knee high. Tomato plants were starting their climbs up the lead strings to the rafters in the high tunnel. Cilantro was well into its name change to coriander as it shifted its focus from leaves to seeds.

Other ripple effects were happening as well. Another WWOOFer, named Caroline, was leaving today after a really enjoyable week we had working together. She was about to start an internship dismantling coal plants. A mechanical engineering student at the University of Kansas, she told me there was not one person majoring in petroleum engineering in her department, that all the best jobs with the most pay and competition were in renewables. Her boyfriend, whom she met years ago at a summer camp where they attended and then worked (which is on the very small amount of authentic tall grass prairie in the state), had a job restoring wetlands this summer.

Caroline and I went to Pawnee Rock together (the actual rock in the little town with the same name), an historic high point on these flat plains that was the mid-point of the Santa Fe Trail and a key vantage point for seeing seemingly-endless bison, wagon trains, tribal movement and gorgeous prairie vistas.

People had carved their names in the soft stone as they passed and wrote about it poetically in their journals (maybe even while skipping school, like someone else we all know). It was now a view of ugly industrial farms. We shifted our minds' eyes as best as we could and imagined what they saw back then. I wondered what it will look like years after Caroline's class graduates, what ripple effect there will be from their forward-thinking focus.

New people were coming soon, and I'd be shifting from my WWOOFing Ritz three-bedroom house to a one-room Walden-esque cabin so that they could use the much larger space I had been inhabiting. I was looking forward to the change, still remembering with fondness the tiny home where I stayed during my pilot test in Mableton, Georgia.

Terra and James would be away for a few days visiting an intentional community. They had dreams of starting their own homestead some day and wanted to check it out — it was a pilot test, of sorts. I was looking forward to hearing about it when they returned and was grateful they would be back a day or so before it was time for me to leave.

More changes were happening. The sun had shifted, no longer rising directly outside my front door but just enough to the left that I had to reposition my focus to locate it. My view was shifting on many other things as well, and locking in more definitively on things I thought to be true and now know to be certain.

There was a ripple effect to my stay, and to this journey *Round America with a Duck*, of course. I wasn't quite sure what it was just yet, but it was happening both outside and inside me.

My ducks, of course, were simply enjoying the puddles.

I was walking next to Lillian, the older of the two Filipino American nurses who were now living in my house after I moved to the tiny cabin. We were heading out to the labyrinth, long overgrown, with the intention of reviving it.

The cross-axis of the Charters-style 11-circuit path had already been marked by Sister Jane and Lila, and Sister Jane already had the lawn mower out there waiting. A permaculture group was coming the next weekend (although I would be at my next farm workstay in Colorado by then), and then a Peace Camp for kids immediately after that. It would be good for this to be ready.

Linda, the other nurse, and Lillian were more used to assisting in cutting open people's chests for cardiac surgery on life-saving missions all over the world (18 countries and counting) rather than cutting open hay bales to feed alpacas, yet they proved to be conscientious and committed workers from the moment they arrived two days prior. They blew threw tasks in record speed, were game for anything (including hula hooping with me in the barn loft and joining in our alpaca fleece dryer-ball-making party for the gift shop), and asked many questions.

It was my turn to ask a question (although I had already asked these fascinating women a lot of them).

"Where are you going next?" I asked Lillian, who walked quite a bit slower than Linda. (She would peacefully say, "I'm coming" when I would check to make sure she was okay — especially on the long walks bringing the alpacas out to the range — or I would slow my own pace to meet hers.)

Lillian answered simply, "Where the Lord sends me next."

I took that in for a moment. It's a good answer. One I say to myself, in different words, as part of my daily sunrise meditation.

"How will you know?" I asked.

"I will get a sign," she replied.

The labyrinth challenge proved too much for us that day. Sister Jane and I ended up out there for hours, blazed by the sun and bit by bugs (Lillian, Linda and Lila eventually returning to the weeding and other tasks back in the gardens after chopping some trees).

We had twisted and turned the map and our bodies. We made lawn mower mistakes that would require weeks of fresh new grass growth to correct. We walked and re-walked our broken path but could not find our way forward just yet. We, in fact, did not know where the Lord wanted us. When Sister Jane suggested perhaps we break for a little nibble, I leaped on it. God wanted us to snack. That much was clear.

Neither of us ever mentioned going back. Perhaps we were waiting for a sign.

At the weekly staff meeting, at which WWOOFers were included, Tre mentioned that there was a cyclist named Mike passing through who would be staying at Hedge House for two nights. This five-bedroom house was the available-for-rent guest house next to the chicken coop.

My ears perked up at this. It would be fun to talk with another bike rider, especially a person bike touring, which was different from what I was doing and was increasingly something I saw as a possibility in my future, now that I was becoming so smitten with our country and the good experiences I was having, tornado aside. Plus, I was hoping to WWOOF around the world, and many other countries make it easier for bike touring.

I ran into Mike when Sister Jane was giving him a tour of the farm. I told him I'd be feeding the alpacas soon, if he was interested in watching or helping. He came and loved it, and ended up helping me put the chickens to bed that night and bring the alpacas out to the range the next day. He did a handful of other things around the farm as well. Built benches. Repaired the high tunnel's door. Climbed a huge ladder to open the windows in the octagonal cob straw-bale building (after telling me he was experiencing a bit of vertigo recently, unbeknownst to the Sisters).

We chatted a lot. I knew he was traveling from New Mexico to Wisconsin or so, about 50 or 60 miles/80 or 96 kilometers a day — 600 miles/966 kilometers already in the prior two weeks. I knew he intended to be gone for about two months. I knew his son was posting Mike's handwritten journal entries on a blog. I knew he was mistaken for a homeless man a few days ago and someone left him food outside his tent.

I knew he did a similar long-distance trip (from Minneapolis to New York) in 1977, and he was now 67 years old. That he recently retired from his job as a hydrologist working to find suitable sites for nuclear waste disposal and evaluating aquifer health. That he was a Veteran of the Vietnam War, having served in the US Air Force. That he never stopped riding his bike throughout the years.

I knew he liked to sing while riding his bike on endless open roads, sometimes songs from a family music tape to which he and his kids used to listen, like "I've Been Working on the Railroad." Sometimes ear worms he picked up from some stop along the way, like the time he couldn't get the song "Ta Ra Ra Boom Dee Ay" out of his mind. Sometimes Paul Simon's timeless lament on the American experience, "American Tune," which he sang for me on the open dirt road in front of our farm right before departing.

*I don't know a soul who's not been battered*
*I don't have a friend who feels at ease*
*I don't know a dream that's not been shattered*
*Or driven to its knees*

As he was packing up, loading his bike with his four water bottles, one day's worth of food, a change of clothes, a small tent and sleeping mat, flip flops, and sunscreen, I asked him, as I ask everyone, if he had hope. His answer shook me, not from shock but from recognition of its truth.

"It's too late, you know," he said, referring to the world's sixth great extinction, currently underway. He said that even if all emissions stopped today, it was still too late.

"I know," I replied, sadly. Even those of us who consider ourselves optimists were having trouble denying that. "But hope? There's always hope, right? Or if not hope, what gives you peace?"

He believed in reincarnation, he told me, and that he would come back in some form someday.

"There's no escaping the wheel," he said.

And then he rode away.

When I tapped in to see what he wrote about Heartland Farm (nice things), I noticed at the top of his blog that he titled his journey *The End of Life As We Know It Midwest Tour*.

Truth? I was a little worried about Mike.

And us.

And now it was *my* turn to start to pack. My throat choked as I removed my *You're Enough* sweatshirt from the clothesline. How could I leave here? Would I ever be enough again anywhere else?

"You don't have to go, you know," Christi had said to me when she took me to meet her cows and then gave me a tour of downtown

Great Bend — its art, its zoo — as we ate frozen yogurt in waffle cones together. I had been to the supermarket several times as well as the Mother House, but I hadn't really seen much else of the city so this was fun.

I had seen every acre of this sanctuary, however, and yet it wasn't enough. I rode its every corner on my bike one last time, risking yet another flat from the locust and goat head thorns. Down one grassy path beyond a one-room cob straw house named The Hermitage, there was a large patch of hemp, much smaller than what the farmer was growing next to Lish's farm in North Carolina, but hemp just the same.

Sister Jane confirmed what I had heard about hemp while in North Carolina, that during World War II, farmers were asked to plant it to use to make ropes for warships after Japan cut off our country's usual supply of Filipino hemp and Indian jute. It is technically illegal to grow hemp now because it's a member of the cannabis family (despite its many uses beyond its very low level of THC as a recreational and medicinal drug) but many farms still had remnants like right here on this land owned by the Dominican Sisters of Peace. I made a little TikTok about this, my first ever to be removed as a violation of community guidelines.

On my way back to the main part of the farm, I lingered at the Hermitage. Completely off the grid, it's a one-room haven for solitude, and the guest log attests to the transformational experiences that mostly-solo travelers have had here since 1991.

I sat in the fading light of day on a small concrete bench overlooking a forested creek, hoping to finally spot armadillos, which I had heard were common here, and read through the entries of those whose feet have passed this way before me.

I finally said my goodbyes to this land and prepared to say goodbye to these people who had welcomed me so fully and unconditionally. They were living proof to me that the principle of radical non-judgment I adopted in North Carolina, with healthy boundaries as learned in Missouri, could be a sustainable practice for the rest of my life.

The fine folks at Heartland Farm threw me a going-away lunch, and both Christi and I cried. Sister Imelda gave me a balm it takes her a year to make because it requires her to soak certain wild plants — plantain, chickweed and yarrow — in oil over time.

"It's for itches and scratches ahead for you on your journey," she told me. I looked into her gorgeous 85-year-old face and tried to memorize her. *Would I ever pass this way again?*

I thought of Bernard asking me to paint his bike in New York City. The possibility of a desk clerk job at the hotel in Joplin, Missouri. And now there was Kansas to add to my *what-if* ennui. Should I just stay? Was this God's plan? Would my husband like Kansas — or was this *our* fork in the road? This journey was making one thing abundantly clear. There are so many ways to live a life. When do we stay and when do we go?

Over the years, you wonder, sometimes, if you or your spouse is going to fall in love with someone else. It happens to many couples, especially after the kids leave the house, as ours had. You get to decide what your encore years are going to be like, and if you are going to stay together for them. This journey was a risk, as we knew, and I did, indeed, fall in love. At first I thought it was with Kansas — but, perhaps, it was with who I was in Kansas. Was there a way to bring the parts of me I loved home and to leave the parts of me I didn't along the way?

Like the Filipino nurses, I looked for a sign telling me where the Lord wanted me next as I was finishing packing while listening to Momma's Adventure Playlist. And then I heard these lines from the song "Fever Dream":

*How far away can I walk*
*'Til I'm way too far from home?*

I somehow knew deep in my bones that I wasn't done yet with wherever it was that my bike and trains and buses were taking me. I wasn't done becoming, and shedding.

I strapped on my backpack, took one last look around the cabin, cursed that composting toilet (which I hadn't used for the past four days so Sister Jane would not end up on the roof again — thank goodness for the nearby art studio's bathroom), stepped out the door, and twirled with my backpack as Willie Nelson sang his song.

I was on the road again, and I did not look back. How long would this resolve to continue last?

# 5

## Time Makes You Bolder

I can't tell you how happily I was doing my little dance in front of a fast food joint in tiny Ellis, Kansas. A day or two before I left Heartland Farm, I had discovered that the bus company added a stop there, which replaced the one that was suspended in Hays nearby. Therefore, I needed to only go one hour to Ellis rather than two hours to Wichita, and I changed my bus ticket to reflect this.

Lila had generously offered to drive me to Wichita, but she was thrilled we were going to Ellis instead, not only because it was closer but also because she loved the library in Hays and we would pass it on our way to Ellis and had time to stop.

The bus was scheduled for 5:45 in the morning, so I decided to book a hotel the night before — the same hotel chain as in Joplin — and planned to spend a stress-free evening just relaxing. Lila and I enjoyed the library. There was even a seed library there! I found out afterwards that there was a trail in Hays that goes right past a herd of bison. There was really an endless amount of things to see and do and learn in this country, in this world, even in the smallest of places — maybe even *especially* there. I would soon find out in Ellis.

Lila dropped me off at the hotel and we hugged goodbye. I got a sundae at the Love's truck stop across the street, a major place of business here in this small 2,000-resident town. I texted my brother about how it reminded me of when we stayed at this hotel chain growing up and got ice cream at McDonald's. Then, I walked over to the bus stop to make sure I had the right location.

It was clearly marked with a branded bus sign. To be truly certain, I confirmed it with the night manager at the hotel, who verified that I had it right. He added that it was a new stop and they were very excited about it since it was the only one for many miles and they hoped it would increase room stays here. Feeling great, relaxed, and happy, I slept soundly.

I got up at 3:00 AM, wrote a bit, and then discovered it was raining. *Please, God, no tornado. Not today, okay?* I prayed. I put on my rain gear, checked out of the hotel, and rolled my bike filled with my stuff across the street and down the block to the curb where the bus stop was. I folded up my bike and packed up the bike bag and settled in. I opened my umbrella over my stuff and waited.

And then I got a notification that the bus was going to be late, first one hour, updated a while later to two hours. It was honestly too much work to pack everything up again, haul my oats back to the hotel just to sit and then maneuver my way back here, so

I just decided to stay put. I could read. I could meditate. I could make TikToks.

Eventually, I had to pee. This is when I made the remarkable discovery that my rain poncho completely covered me and *I could now pee anywhere*, including right there on the curb. This was life-changing, folks. If you saw any photos of me from other places sitting by a curb or in a park wearing a rain poncho on sunny days, now you know why.

All was well.

*Until it wasn't.*

At 7:45 AM sharp on that first Friday in June, I saw the bus bound for Denver get off I-70 on Washington Street in Ellis, Kansas and never make the right hand turn on Jefferson to go the short way to the official bus stop.

I got that nagging knot in my stomach any time I feel like I'm being forgotten but then remembered how the bus driver had stopped in Greensburg, North Carolina to move the bus to get gas, scaring everyone who was still in the gas station into thinking they were being left behind. *Maybe the bus driver is getting gas at the truck stop first before coming to get me*, I thought, breathing in, breathing out, trying to neutralize my learned trauma response.

And then I saw the bus go in the opposite direction back to the highway. I watched it barrel on down the interstate and fade into the distance. It wasn't coming back. It wasn't coming to get me. The driver forgot me.

The knot in my stomach rose up into my throat and the tears came quickly. I just sat there on the curb in front of the fast food joint in my little puddle of pee and cried and cried and cried. I was five years old again. Six. Seven. Eight.

I caught my breath and told myself I was okay. I was okay. *I was okay.* It was daylight now. I was somewhere safe. I figured out The Tin Can in North Carolina and I figured out Joplin and I could figure this out, too. It was just another challenge, another pivot. Trust the journey, right?

The bus sign said, "Where is my bus?" It had a number to call, so I did. The person who answered told me my bus had already passed, which, of course, I knew. When I explained that the driver had missed the stop, he said he could not do anything about that.

"The bus isn't coming back for you, if that's what you're suggesting," he stated.

When I asked how the bus company was going to make this right, he said I needed to send an email to customer service.

"What about being re-booked?" I asked. "Can you do that?"

He said, "We're not responsible for schedule delays. You'll need to book a new trip yourself."

"But this wasn't a schedule delay," I replied, realizing we were about to go in circles.

"I can't help you," he said.

*Breathe in. Breathe out. You can do this*, I told myself.

I already had to rebook my trip in Oklahoma City after the missed connection because the clerk kept insisting the bus was still coming (which it wasn't) and he wouldn't rebook it for me, and I was concerned I would lose a spot on the one-bus-a-day the next day. And now, it was happening again that I was going to be on the line for un-budgeted costs that should have been covered by the bus company. I had him book a brand new trip for me. Cha-ching, cha-ching. Any money I was hoping to use in cities was continually getting blown on things like this, in case you are wondering why I never rave about any restaurants or tourist attractions on this journey.

So, a seat secured for tomorrow, I decided to go back to the hotel. I had paid for the room through 11:00 AM so I would just go up there and figure things out a bit. I unpacked my bike, snapped it open, loaded it up and trudged back across the busy main road to the hotel. This journey sometimes felt like one big trudge, shlep, haul.

I told the desk clerk what had happened. She was surprised. I then asked if I could go back to my room for a while, and she shook her head no. "You already checked out and it's already being cleaned," she replied. I should have seen that coming, but I was still shocked.

And then it got worse.

I said, "Well, I need to book a new room anyway for tonight, so how about we do that? I can work in the lobby until it's ready."

She glanced at her computer and then looked up reluctantly.

"We're actually fully booked for tonight," she said, sadly.

Fully booked? *Breathe. Breathe. Breathe.*

"Is there another hotel nearby?"

She slowly shook her head no.

She could clearly tell I was doing everything I could to hold it together. In an obvious act of mercy, she tapped into her computer for a moment and then handed me a room card.

"This is for the conference room. It's completely empty right now and locked. It's now *your* room for as long as you need it today. I'm going to figure out how to make this work."

And so, yes again, folks, we are reminded that there is a God, and there is good, and there is hope.

I let my husband know that I now lived in Ellis, Kansas, possibly forever, as I didn't know if the bus would ever stop here. Oh, and I would most likely be tent-camping — could Amazon same-day deliver one tonight like it did with Smiley in North Carolina? Good thing I knew how to squat.

I spent a solid hour composing my detailed email to the bus company's customer service address. To this day, I have never heard back from them. I did, however, hear from that lovely lady at the front desk later that morning. She had secured me a room.

What's more, she spoke to the night manager, the one who had made the deal with the bus company about the bus stop. He told her I needed to see a guy who knew the guy who was the regional manager for the bus company and could "take care of things." The guy who knew the guy apparently hung out in a back booth at the fast food joint, where the bus stop was. I had to get lucky and cross paths with him at precisely the right moment.

Could I make this stuff up? No. No, I could not.

So I headed back over to the fast food joint and asked the first cashier I saw if she knew the guy I needed to see. She pointed to the back booth, and there he was with the hotel's night manager! Sure enough, he connected me with Ben, the right guy at the bus company, who then made sure I got compensated for my extra hotel night. Ben also contacted the bus driver to make sure he knew he had a passenger the next morning. *Me.*

I was back on track. My husband, who was frantically searching for alternative transportation options, of which there were none, had been considering driving out to get me. We both realized that I was now beyond what we had been calling the turn-back point. There was nowhere to go but forward.

I had now been gifted with what I called my Bonus Day in Ellis. *Why did my Higher Power want me to be here this day?* I wondered. I needed to go find out.

A storm moved quickly toward us. I only had an hour, if that much, before it would downpour, and the possibility of a tornado was a threat I didn't want to face again. But I needed a bike ride desperately. It was not only important for me physically but mentally, and the prior 24 hours had been a lot. As my hit-and-run survival near my home made clear, we make life-and-death decisions every time we leave our homes on a bike, and this was just another one of them.

I rode through charming Ellis, down Main Street and past the community co-op, which I had learned from my time in Kansas (never having seen these before) is where farmers go to sell their harvested grain and get seed, feed and other supplies. These are the silos you see alongside train tracks in many small country towns. The trains would take those grains to big cities for sale.

I turned the corner on my bike and came upon a stunning church, ominous clouds hanging heavy over it. People dressed in black were leaving, and a black and silver hearse sat in front. I took a photo and liked the perspective of it — the dark, the light, the mood, the lines.

My perspective had changed. Yes, I had a Bonus Day in Ellis, I realized. But I also had a Bonus Day in *life*. In fact, I had one every day. I needed to remember that.

Maybe at my age I had already done everything I was born to do in life. I had planted some seeds of change in my community. My husband and I had built a bridge to the future with our daughters. Perhaps at this point everything was bonus time, and I was just here to bear witness, to spread joy as an act of resistance to the pervasive negativity that surrounds us, and to help in other small ways when needed. It's possible my remaining purpose and meaning weren't any more complicated than that.

The next morning, which was World Bicycle Day, I packed up my carefully-curated travel items, including my folding bike, along with a side sack of worry that the bus wouldn't stop for me again. I said goodbye to the desk clerk, again, and made my way back over to the bus stop at 3:58 AM.

I sat there under the street light, a woman alone, in the dark of early morning, thinking big thoughts. *What kind of bus stop is this? Why are we treating people in our country — women, children, people with disabilities — like this? Why is it so hard to travel across America with dignity, dependability and safety? Why is my only choice to pee on the curb?*

I had heard someone say that there were two words that changed her life.

*For now.*

Whenever she had an uncomfortable feeling, she added those words to it to help remind her that this too shall pass.

I was trying desperately, often unsuccessfully, to remember that I was exactly where I was meant to be, even if I felt vulnerable.

For now.

No wind turbines. I kept waiting for them to appear, as they had when I first entered Kansas on that bus from Oklahoma City, but there were none. I had been overwhelmed by their beauty, having never seen one in person before. They gave me hope and even made me teary when I thought of their potential. So close to the highway, they practically touched the bus.

I had loved learning all about them from Terra's spouse, James, who had just become certified as a wind turbine technician. But now, finally on the bus out of Ellis, in front of which I had whooped and hollered with joy when it finally arrived, I peered out the window waiting, but no wind turbines appeared.

Maybe the wind turbines I had seen in Eastern Kansas were a fleeting thing that I would never see again on this journey — a reminder, of course, that every moment was precious.

Elise, my WWOOF host in Boulder, had been texting me for weeks asking what kind of food I liked and other thoughtful questions pertaining to my upcoming three-week stay with her. In fact, she was a big part of why I kept going after Joplin.

First, she had been so kind to me during my moments of turmoil in the hotel trying to figure out what to do next. Second, the fact that she had already started stocking a cupboard for me with my preferred food items made me feel indebted to her in many good ways. And now, I was finally on my way to Pleasant Ridge Organics right on the northern border of the City of Boulder.

However much I enjoyed my dirt-road bike rides in Kansas and my little rides with Peanut in North Carolina, I loved city riding, as Philly and New York City reminded me, and Boulder was renowned for its bike infrastructure so I was especially excited. I would be working on Elise's "farmette," as she referred to it in her WWOOF profile, for five hours a day six days a week, but the rest of the time was mine to explore.

PeopleForBikes, for whom I served as a national ambassador, had its headquarters there. I had even interviewed and written a profile about its president and CEO, Jenn Dice, as part of my *You Go, Girl* series of 31 articles (one each day in August 2020) featuring women making it more welcoming to ride bikes, which I wrote as part of my healing process after surviving that hit-and-run on my bike a mile from my home.

I was looking forward to the farm work as well. Elise's farmette was just two acres/less than one hectare but it sounded like a lot happened there. She referred to being part of a CSA, which stands for Community Supported Agriculture, which is when people pre-order and receive a box of produce each week throughout a growing season. I had been a CSA member for many years of multiple Metro Atlanta farms while my daughters were growing up, so I was looking forward to being on the other side of the table.

In addition to raised garden beds and rows of crops, Elise had an orchard. Although I had worked with fruit trees before, and certainly enjoyed foraging from public ones from mulberries through native persimmons (from April through October) while riding my bike around Atlanta, I had much to learn.

Most interestingly, Elise said she was part of a flower program, which would be new to me. I didn't know if she sold directly to consumers or to flower shops, restaurants and other places and I was curious to find out more. I hadn't been big on flower growing during my years starting community, school, refugee, food pantry, home and other gardens, as my focus had always been on growing food, especially for those in need, but the fact that she had monetized small-scale flower-growing caught my attention.

I had been selected as an agribusiness specialist for my Peace Corps Uganda assignment and would have been working with small farmers to create and maximize their income from what's called value-added products. I believed this experience on Elise's farmette would be helpful to me if I were ever to reapply (which wasn't out of the question).

I also knew there was a WWOOF location on an island in Alaska that was the biggest supplier of the world's peonies. After my year working with that state in my communications specialist role with the CDC Foundation, this held interest to me as well (although they said they could not accommodate a vegetarian as they rely so much on seafood). So my farm workstay at Elise's farmette promised to add a new dimension to my cross-country experiences.

I had a little trepidation because folks with whom I had worked before who were into flower-growing seemed to be very particular — maybe flowers necessitated this — and I wasn't. I had learned from many mentors as well as my own extensive experience that there were lots of correct ways to coax life from the soil as an organic grower. I enjoyed the freedom to explore and experiment without shame or blame. In fact, the flower team at the community garden I helped start kept themselves pretty separate from the food growers. We just seemed to know intuitively that we were different from each other in some important ways.

And yet, there I was.

Elise had told me the best place to meet was the Table Mesa stop on the commuter bus line. These comfortable coach buses (there's no train) ran from Boulder to Denver up and down State Route 36 along the Flatirons, which are the foothills of the Rocky Mountains. They departed frequently and cost just a little more than five dollars a trip.

With a folding bike rack on the front and cargo bays underneath, they were the essence of bike-friendliness. I noticed the Boulder to Denver Bikeway outside my window alongside SR 36, like the Wantagh Parkway Path way back on Long Island. I also noticed there were bike storage shelters at stops along the way. I, once again, felt like I had died and gone to heaven, this time for bikes.

The rain was just ending when Elise picked me up and she told me how much rain they had had lately and how odd that was. It apparently looked more like Ireland than Boulder right now. It was truly emerald green in every direction. (Should I rename my book *Round Ireland with a Duck* —or is that still to come in my life?)

Just a year and a half before, a deadly fire killed two people and destroyed more than 1,000 homes, a hotel and a shopping center right here in Boulder and damaged six public drinking water systems. It was the most destructive fire in Colorado history. This extensive rain was now creating even more concern. Fast, abundant vegetation growth in the spring, if followed by intense dry heat in the summer, as expected, would lay the foundation for a tinderbox. The fire department was even going around from neighborhood-to-neighborhood conducting trainings for how to reduce the chance of losing your home to a wildlife. Cue Smokey the Bear.

The rain, of course, had made Elise's gardens lush, but as she showed me around, that's what kept jumping out at me. *This was just a home garden on a semi-suburban street.* Not *just*, as in belittling it, because I know personally how much work a home garden like this takes. My entire home landscape had been a food-growing space for many years, producing thousands of dollars worth of food that my family consumed. I had, in fact, written a 97,000-word book about it titled *Food for My Daughters: what one mom did when the towers fell (and what you can do, too).* But where was the farmette? Where were the agribusiness outreaches?

"What about the CSA?" I asked.

No CSA.

"What about the flower program?" I tried.

No flower program.

"Do you sell crops to restaurants?" I grasped.

"I used to," Elise replied.

My heart sank. Yes, Elise's WWOOF profile was outdated, but the fact that this was a surprise to me was my fault. I didn't ask enough questions when we talked on the phone. I didn't ask for a video chat where I could see the farmette. Elise didn't even have chickens, which would have helped me see this home garden as more of a homestead, and I would have known that had I asked.

In retrospect, I realize I was also perhaps confused. I didn't know home gardeners could join the WWOOF program as hosts. Is this something *I* could do with my home garden? With our rapidly-aging population, and more older folks staying in their large homes, might promoting this non-commercial small-scale workstay option be a way for people to not only learn about home gardening (and help older folks who may not be as physically up to the tasks anymore) but also provide affordable living arrangements for long-term WWOOFers in cities and towns? For WWOOFers who work remotely, this could be a real win-win.

I had such mixed emotions. Luckily, Elise was generous, her home was lovely and the view was breathtaking. I could tell there'd be lots of top-quality food — in addition to the bountiful spring garden, she had filled my cupboard with organic food and welcomed me with wild asparagus soup, and we even got to forage for more asparagus together. My WWOOF accommodations included the best bed of my entire trip and a luxurious private bathroom with one of those heat lamps for when I got out of the shower.

She also had a wonderful old dog named Nina, and I would soon find out, a terrific housemate named Laure, with whom I shared the upstairs apartment (and some meals), took hikes at Chautauqua Park and Wonderland Lake, and hula-hooped in the driveway like with Lillian and Linda in the hay loft in Kansas.

Like a dog — Peanut or Nina perhaps — I needed to pee on a tree, so to speak, to make myself at home (no I didn't actually do this, although I know at this point you don't consider that outside the realm of possibility for me). I needed to ground myself, and that meant a bike ride. And that bike ride would be in *Boulder, Colorado*, I reminded myself. Trust the journey, right? *We may never pass this way again.*

I pedaled along a bucolic country road on the edge of rural life, and then found myself in an upscale suburban area with the kinds of bike lanes and trails about which my city back in Metro Atlanta has been fighting for years now.

I sent a little update to my neighbor-at-home Jason, who is the only other person besides me who rides a bike to city meetings due to the risk required. He told me that our local master trail plan had finally passed. The only city councilor who voted against it was the one featured in a public service campaign I created pro bono years ago for the local bike/walk advocacy group, also used by the statewide advocacy group Georgia Bikes, whose quote said he was is support of making the city bike-friendly because he was a dad and it hit close to home. His kids were grown up now so I guess his view had changed.

My children grown up, too, I realized my view had changed as well. A journey such as this wasn't just about ticking off destinations along the way like a scavenger hunt. It was about making choices every step of the way about how I wanted to move forward, with whom, where, and why. It was about figuring out what was revered — and feared — in our society by experiencing examples from a wide range of communities. And it was about honoring the art of feeling fully alive at a human-scaled pace in a country and world gone haywire.

As my time in Boulder went on, I met people working with the bikeshare program, got my bike tuned up (and thorns picked out of my tires with tweezers) at REI, and explored almost every single street and path. I went to the Boulder Reservoir, closed-to-cars Pearl

Street, the robust farmers market downtown and the breathtaking library straddling Boulder Creek. I patronized a small convenience store that benefits the Meals on Wheels program, dropped off unopened travel-sized toiletries from Elise at the Boulder Homeless Shelter, and bought some new ribbon at a creative reuse store to secure Disco Duck to my handlebars better after almost losing him.

When I popped into supermarkets with my bike folded in the grocery cart, the clerks said things like "that's rad!" and "I love your bike!" That meant a lot coming from Boulderites, where bikes were put on a pedestal and the very best athletes from around the world trained and raced on the most expensive and advanced bikes made, including in an Ironman event during my stay.

There were also people like Annie here. I ran into her when she was flying around for the very first time on her new electric tricycle, smiling broadly. Annie told me she stopped riding a regular bike two years ago because of her knees and that "that wouldn't do," especially while living in a city like Boulder. She said she was going to put a sign on her new trike that read "Wide Load. No Wisecracks!" And then her raucous laugh filled the cottonwood-fluff-dotted air.

My bike rides became a glorious highlight of my days. As I was halfway across a bridge after challenging myself on one of the pump tracks at the astounding Valmont Bike Park one day (where there are 40 acres/16 hectares of trails, jumps, slaloms and tracks), I realized I was exactly halfway *Round America with a Duck*, time-wise. I was halfway missing home and halfway looking forward to what was still left to explore. I was halfway tired and halfway energized, and 100% glad I was still doing this. *How close I came to quitting.*

My daily rides revealed a bit of an underbelly as well. I noticed there were still the same problems as everywhere. Too-narrow unprotected bike lanes suddenly ended. Drivers sped. The number one thing people said to me since I arrived was not to lock my bike anywhere because it would be stolen. And there were increasingly un-housed people, many with mental illness, on the isolated trails, which concerned me as a woman alone. There were many spots without sidewalks and there were still plastic bags at the Safeway supermarket, to which there was no immediately-clear safe way to get on a bike (I made it there anyway, and eventually figured out a good route).

There were significant climate impacts here, just like everywhere I'd been. The daily storms, which every single person I met told me were not normal, meant I had my rain gear on constantly and was seeking cover in tunnels below overpasses with other bike riders. This gave us a chance to chat, and of course, I asked them my routine question. And, yes, like everywhere, they said they had hope, and the loss of hope.

I even kept trying to get to one special place and aborting my mission because of extreme weather. It was, ironically, the National Center for Atmospheric Research.

In short, everything was not peachy in Boulder. In fact, there were many of the same issues from back in the Peach State city that I currently call home (with the exception of them being 20 years ahead on trails in Boulder). A report had just come out in Georgia, by the way, that said 90% of this year's peach crop was lost due to the unseasonably warm winter we just had. A nonprofit farm and education center named Growing Gardens that I had visited here in Boulder lost its entire orchard one night due to hail.

There were other things that concerned me. Elise and I were, indeed, different types of people in the garden, and working shoulder-to-shoulder felt tense. We weren't having fun, and fun matters to me.

At what turned out to be, paradoxically, very pleasant lunches together, I suggested I focus on weeding. There was lots of it to do, I knew which plants were wanted and which weren't, I could do the entire garden before I left plus spread a pile of wood chips, and we could work independently. Elise agreed, and so that's what I did for the rest of my stay there during my WWOOF hours.

Elise loved to teach and I wondered if I frustrated her. I am confident that this WWOOF workstay would be a better fit for folks who want to learn her methods, not that there wasn't much for me to learn. There clearly was. There *always* is. But our work styles just didn't click, and I was struggling internally there, despite the beauty and bounty of it all. It took intense daily focus to stay up-tempo. At my WWOOF pilot-test back in Mableton, Georgia,

I had made a list of lessons learned. The very first one was to take care of my needs unapologetically. And so, I did. For me, that meant setting an alarm for when my work hours ended and hopping on that bike rain or shine.

To be fair, we are all navigating our way back to a new sense of normal after COVID, and there are likely to be bumps, not just in the accuracy of WWOOF profiles. Elise did invite me during my stay to numerous local farmer gatherings and even a talk by the former editor-in-chief of *Gourmet* magazine, Ruth Reichl, who is a food-world icon, but I passed on these due to my COVID-safe commitment to myself. Those may have been great experiences for us to share.

I did enjoy visiting various nearby farms on my bike rides, however, and I even found a volunteer gig for after my WWOOF hours. While riding my bike, I had been passing a sign each day just up the road from Elise's home that said "Earth's Table." I looked them up and they were doing good work for those in need, the kind of work my friends and I used to do at our community and food pantry gardens. The kind of work I left behind at my beloved refugee garden. I knew it was time to elevate what I was doing here in Boulder.

So I reached out to the retired pastor who led this group of volunteers to grow food at various Boulder-area gardens and farms, 100% of which is donated. Le Jardin Francaise. Marpa. Jubilee. Wonderview. Plumbumpy (what a fun name). And generically-named Garden #9, which was the one I passed each day. They've received thousands of volunteer hours and donated tens of thousands of pounds of culturally-appropriate vegetables — hot pepper, tomatillos, tomatoes and more — over the past eight years or so.

Pete and I were immediately simpatico. I completely got what he was doing and how, and his style was similar to mine so I felt more open to learning. Burlap coffee bean bags from the local roastery lining the paths? I hadn't seen that. Cool. I told him about the alpaca fleece to suppress weeds in the paths at the farm where I WWOOFed previously. We talked about epazote, a Mexican mint favored by the population we served, which was similar to his.

He said the brome grass from the ranch that was on the land prior to him being there keeps invading. I told him how the alpacas love that. He said, "So I should get an alpaca?"

I replied, "Well, they are herd animals so you need a bunch."

I honestly think he considered it for a moment!

Together we carried and hammered in tall wooden poles up and down a row of tomatoes and weaved yucca twine throughout them to support the coming bounty. I hadn't done that before.

We talked. We laughed. I felt more whole, more authentically myself, just from that hour there. I went back two more times.

I learned this lesson: If you don't feel like you are fulfilling your calling or using your valuable skillset as broadly or deeply as your heart and soul needs, ask yourself how you can elevate your choices. How can you rise above the reality that is presented to you wherever you are in life and create your own new way forward?

As Earth's Table's tagline said, *the end of hunger starts here.* Perhaps the end of hungering for a more elevated life starts here, too. Right now. Today. For me. For you. For all of us. How will we choose, or continue to choose, to rise to the uniquely unrepeatable gift of time that is our life?

I knew it was time to venture beyond the borders of Boulder, and my day off had a rare weather forecast mostly without rain, so I decided to ride to Denver.

I was about 35 miles/56 kilometers into my bike ride on the Boulder to Denver Bikeway directly beside US Highway 36 when it suddenly ended, dumping me in a park in a town named Westminster. I wandered aimlessly for a while, happy to discover a sculpture garden and numerous murals. I then took some random multi-use path and tried to intuit my way forward. At some point I glanced down, and that's when I realized Disco Duck was gone!

I retraced my pedals frantically trying to find him, panicked but already visualizing my "Find Disco!" flyer. All of America would rally to find Disco! Maybe that's exactly what we needed in this country to start to work together again.

Alas, I found him. He was lying there in a gutter on a busy road, and I scooped him up and kissed his little head. He wouldn't save the country just yet.

I then crap-shot my way forward again, taking this path and that, stopping often to pull out my glasses and pop open my phone, hello vulnerable woman alone, when walkers misdirected me and I got snarled in a vortex of lost.

Enter Batman! I actually met two men on bikes named Bruce and Wayne, the first and last names of Batman's alias. I evaluated the level of threat they might be to me and decided the threat of being lost and alone in an isolated area was worse.

I asked them, "How do I get to Denver?" and they told me to follow them. We rode together for about 12 miles/19 kilometers, through what I guessed (and confirmed later) was the armpit of Denver, dump and all.

I almost always ride alone, and it was so different to be riding with guys (I notice this as well when I occasionally ride with some of my guy friends at home). I didn't need to be scanning left and right or looking over my shoulder continually for potential attackers. I didn't need to stop, turn around and re-route when things looked sketchy. I didn't need to hold my u-lock as a weapon or have my phone pre-dialed to 911. I just got to ride. How different it was to navigate the world like that.

On the other hand, I didn't get a second to stop and take photos of some really beautiful art and the largest oil refinery in the Rocky

Mountain region because these guys were rockin', but I appreciated them in this circumstance. In fact, I wouldn't have been able to get to Denver without them due to the multiple dangers.

We ended our ride together at Commons Park, and it was our first time actually talking in any detail. They were blown away that I could keep up with them on my little 20-inch wheels. They assumed they would have lost me ages ago, having even told me at the beginning to just make sure the Platte River was always on my right. They didn't know I pedaled my heart out because my life depended on it.

"Where did you start?" they asked.

"Boulder," I replied.

"You didn't start in Boulder," one insisted.

"I did," I said.

"You went up that big hill?" the other asked, incredulously.

Boulder is in a valley, and yes, you have to climb out of it. Yes, it's a big hill.

"I did."

I danced, in fact, at the top of that hill. I made a TikTok (of course).

And that was that. I thanked them for helping me, and we said goodbye. I then peed nonchalantly under my skirt while crouching down and pretending I was fixing something on my bike tire.

As I was riding more on the South Platte River Path and the converging Cherry Creek Path, I found a mural of . . . Batman! What were the chances of that?

After visiting the most beautiful REI ever right there where the two waterways met, I swung by the tail end of the Denver Nuggets championship parade and caught the street cleaners sucking up confetti. I explored the 16th Street Mall outdoor avenue, where apparently a very large, transformative construction project was under way. And having already eaten all my snacks — oranges, nuts, a protein bar and a hunk of cheese — I bought chocolate-covered raisins for my bus ride back to Boulder.

I swung through gorgeous Union Station and saw where my train would leave in a few days, making me feel comfortable about that upcoming departure. I then hopped on the bus, my folding bike stored in the bay underneath, and got off at Table Mesa. The Foothills Parkway Path took me six miles/10 kilometers back to Pleasant Ridge Organics, with the added joy of watching prairie dogs (who apparently spread plague) pop their heads out of the holes along the way. I even got caught in the rain and met yet more nice strangers under a bridge.

"Hope? Do you feel hope?" I asked, as usual.

Some yes's. Some no's. As usual.

Then, I got a text from my husband showing a photo of part of the Father's Day gift I sent him. It was a Batman duck! We were in the middle of watching all the original *Batman* episodes together when I left for this journey. He had given me Disco's side duck. My older daughter had just named the side duck a day or two before, by the way. She named them Robin. Batman's sidekick. Seems obvious now, but it was a revelation.

I ended the day drenched and happy with my personal-best daily ride record of 50 miles/80 kilometers.

I felt like a superhero.

A woman I knew named Diana lived in Boulder and we had been planning on connecting while I was there. She had served on the sustainability commission that I was appointed to start when where I live in Metro Atlanta became the newest city in the United States in 2008. Our times serving on the commission did not cross, however, but she was particularly supportive of my sustainability initiatives on LinkedIn, as I was hers. Her job empowered her to repurpose toxic brownfields for clean uses, often as community greenspaces, and her posts always gave me hope. Diana, a woman I had never met in person, had even offered for me to stay at her home if I ran into troubles securing a WWOOF stay here.

My time there in Boulder was now drawing to an end, and I was grateful Diana invited me to meet her at a member-owned farm named The Golden Hoof, where she belonged. Riding my bike down Jay Road on the worst of the bike lanes I experienced in

Boulder, I passed farms named Benevolence and Juicy Berry; a water resource recovery facility; and the Walden Ponds Wildlife Habitat.

I wondered what it was like for Diana to live here in comparison to where she used to live, where I *still* live. She and her husband raised their family here. She rides her bike to the enormous farmers market in downtown Boulder each Saturday, where the bike parking area takes up an entire lot. *There are so many ways to live a life.*

The day before I left Boulder, I got a text from a big organization asking me if I would consider running for mayor of my city. While finishing spreading that enormous pile of wood chips wheelbarrow by wheelbarrow, and then on my final daily bike ride around Boulder on Fourmile Canyon Creek, Wonderland Creek and Boulder Creek Trails, I pondered this idea.

Was that my next step after I got home? Was that what I meant by trust the journey — trusting *whatever* the journey presented? Just like with the possibilities of painting Bernard's bike or moving to the alpaca farm in Kansas, there were lots of ways to live a life. The questions, ever present during this journey, kept reverberating. How do we know which is the right road? Or do we just keep choosing haphazardly, like Yogi Berra's saying *when you get to a fork in the road, take it*?

I decided to do what Lillian, the nurse in Kansas, suggested. I would look for a sign.

The next sign I passed said *Welcome to Boulder. 20 MPH Speed Limit.* There were Vision Zero and 20 mile-per-hour signs everywhere. That's a speed limit that saves lives. Would that be possible where I lived? On several of the roads with the too-narrow unprotected bike lanes, there were signs indicating improvements to safety for bike riders and pedestrians were about to start. Could I finally blast through the inertia and greenwashing in the place my husband and I currently call home and help deliver some of the realities I had experienced in Boulder?

Elise and I sat on the porch overlooking the Flatirons, watching the lightning and rain long enough that we also got to enjoy a rainbow.

I thought of *The Wizard of Oz* again, and how I was almost the Wicked Witch on her bike in a tornado in Kansas. I hoped Elise didn't think I was a wicked witch here. I felt a growing softness toward her, and a gratitude that she had opened her home to me. I hoped I had helped lighten her load for a short while out there in that garden, and that the work I had done there enhanced her bounty yet to come.

She shared some vulnerabilities with me that night, aging woman to aging woman, and I believed, perhaps, that I had made a new friend for life. I hoped, as women, we could celebrate our differences and hold each other up. This was not always as easy as it sounds.

Elise was five years older than I am, but we were from the same generation. Women of our generation were not raised to be collaborative with other women. We were all still discovering that we have a world-changing power when we work together. I saw that in Kansas, how the Sisters have spent their lifetimes relying on each other, combining their strengths, trusting each other. Maybe that's what I fell in love with so much.

I met so many powerful women on this journey, and one of the most powerful was next. But, first, I had an upcoming two-night stay in Salt Lake City. My friend Marcelle had texted me when I got to Boulder to let me know she would not be able to meet me there, so I was on my own again. As of 5:00 AM the next morning, I was, as Willie sang, on the road again.

# 6

## Altars and Halters

I would like to tell you there was not another bus issue but, alas, there was. The first-of-the-day commuter bus — the one I needed to catch in order to make it to Denver's Union Station at my desired time to not feel rushed packing and checking my bike bag and backpack — did not come. I didn't panic this time, knowing I had options. Knowing I just needed to pivot. But that meant I needed to call a rideshare service, and that meant $47.96 instead of five bucks and change. Cha-ching, cha-ching.

And thus the pattern on this journey regarding my budget continued, blown yet again due to transportation failures. A couple of the situations — the rideshare in Philly and one yet to come in New Orleans — were times I was originally intending to ride my bike to my hostels but because my trains were significantly delayed and it was then late at night, I had to pay the "woman tax," which means use rideshare instead of walk or ride my bike. Of course, women are sometimes sexually assaulted by rideshare drivers, so there was that to worry about as well.

Spending the night in train stations, with the exception of that layover in Indianapolis (which, admittedly, was sketchy), was not a viable option for me, not only because the stations could be creepy but many times they closed overnight or were located in third-party locations, such as that gas station in Joplin or the A&W fast food joint in Ellis, Kansas. Overnighting was not a choice for anyone, male or female.

My driver that morning in Boulder was a woman named Michelle, and I breathed a sigh of relief when she pulled up. I've never had an issue with a male driver, but having a woman was just one less thing to worry about. It's hard to explain how on edge these travel days made me ever since Joplin, Oklahoma City, and Ellis. The fact that there was usually only one bus or train a day going to my destinations made the stakes even higher that no part of my logistics plan fell apart. I didn't really have additional time or energy for an abduction.

I'm happy to report Denver worked out like a charm. And, as usual, once I was settled in onboard, whether it was a bus or train, I could relax and enjoy myself. This particular train boasted one of the very best routes in the whole passenger rail system as it blazed a path through the Rocky Mountains and past enormous red rock formations.

The panoramic viewing car was full at all times, and, in fact, had a period of time during the day when only the higher-class sleeper car people could use it. Those of us in coach class got plenty of time, however. We went through a historic tunnel and passed a clothing-optional resort. There was more skin as rafters on the Colorado River constantly mooned us, after which passengers would clap and cheer. It was such a thing that the engineer would frequently remind us that was why this section of the river was nicknamed Moon River.

We got into Salt Lake City around midnight. A woman struggled to get her bags off the train. A young boy helped her. We got to talking as I walked with her off the platform. She was a traveling nurse but she had health problems and had to cut her service short several times. Knee replacement surgery. A new hip. And now she needed another new hip. She was having money problems. She was on her way to live with one of her adult children for a while.

She thought her three children, whom she raised alone, considered her a failure. She started to cry and told me she was not a failure. She said she was a survivor.

We hugged.

A man at the station with no leg watched me closely as I unfolded my bike. I smiled and gave him an orange and we got to talking. His name was John. He told me he was getting a new leg in July. His goal was to ride a bike.

I got to my studio apartment where people I don't even know left a key for me under the mat. I rode my bike around this Mormon city and noticed it was covered with Pride flags and had parks that had the fewest rules listed for any park I'd ever been in anywhere. Even a notice about visiting the most sacred space in their religion said there was no dress code. Everyone seemed to be welcome here.

Just like with Elise's childhood home, I rode my bike past my friend Marcelle's old house (instead of going to the Great Salt Lake since it was 104 degrees Fahrenheit/40 degrees Celsius, the bike route there was dangerous, and a rideshare driver told me no driver would come back to get me since it was basically a cesspool). I sent Marcelle photos and a video of her block and school and the mountain that she saw every day for 18 years, and she was so happy about it. I had so many questions and we texted like crazy. I felt like I knew so much more about her after that. Nothing about the Great Salt Lake could have possibly been greater.

I danced in front of art murals and up a staircase painted in rainbow colors. I patronized a fabulous local food shop in a repurposed gas station, and I left my BikeBloom earrings as free art nearby. I waved. People waved back. We laughed together. We ended up caring maybe just a little bit more about each other's welfare. In every city I visited, I did this same sort of thing. Rinse, repeat. It was becoming routine, and yet filled with new surprises unique to each location. I was always on high alert, but I tried to lead with love, and that was taking me places I never imagined.

Next stop, Hare Krishna. Of all the places where I was scheduled to WWOOF, this one caught people's attention the most when I told them about it, and for good reason. Combine a Gaudiya Vaishnava Hindu religious organization with the largest llama rental facility in Utah, drop it into a 90% Mormon community, and tell me that's not interesting. I thought about how more than one person asked me if I wasn't concerned about joining a cult.

And now, I was on the road again. The commuter train (with the best bike car of the journey) took me to Provo, where Caru, my WWOOF co-host with his wife, Vai, told me to catch the 822 bus and just tell the driver to drop me at the temple between Spanish Fork and Salem. So I did. And that's how I ended up surrounded by the Wasatch Mountains on the side of South State Road with mating llamas staring at me with their ears pinned back ready to spit.

I laughed when I saw them, their big, goofy faces hanging over the fence. They were enormous compared to Jasper, Joy and especially tiny Quivira in Kansas, and they had their full coats so didn't look like sock puppets like the sheared alpacas did. A handful of them were in this lower pasture for mating purposes and had been out there for about a month, I was soon to find out.

We would be re-integrating them back into the herd while I was there, which was a whole thing where the herd had to determine who was the alpha male again. I had been at the alpaca ranch during breeding as well, but that had lasted just two days. Sister Jane and I had leaned on the wooden railings and watched the alpaca sex acts. I have a video of it set to Donna Summer's *Love to Love You, Baby*, if I must be honest, which I have shared with very few people, out of respect, I guess, for the lovebirds (or, rather, love *herd*).

After taking some photos of my new furry friends and alerting my husband that I had made it to my destination, I rode my bike up the hill, past a field in cultivation, to the enormous, beautiful temple. I thought to myself, yet again: *God grant me the serenity to accept the things I cannot change, the courage to change the things I can, and the wisdom to know the difference. And mostly, may I not be the asshole.*

Leaving my bike outside, I walked inside, tables to my left, a gift shop to my right.

A monk in an orange vestment looked up from the gift shop counter, his eyes warm and sparkly.

"Hi. I'm Pattie," I introduced myself. "I'm here to WWOOF."

"Hi. I'm Radaka," he said. He told me he was visiting from his monastery in India for the summer, as he had done the prior summer.

I reached out to shake his hand, quickly realizing that was probably not proper protocol with a monk, and raised my hands in prayer instead.

"Welcome," he said, smiling. "Have a seat; I'll let Vai know you are here."

He then walked over to the buffet and came back with a cup that he placed in front of me on the table.

"It's lemonade," he said, smiling.

I hadn't realized how hot and thirsty I was. I carried two water bottles with me and drank them constantly, but, especially on travel days, it was easy to get overheated. I wore my heaviest clothes to travel, which meant my jeans, socks, farm shoes and a sweatshirt around my tank-topped waist, and we were now in summer, in the American West, so temperatures were rising rapidly.

An older woman wearing a long skirt and walking with a limp and a cane entered the temple and came over to my table. She stood and looked at me a moment, introduced herself as Vai and then sat down. She asked me what had brought me here, and I told her a bit about my journey so far and why I was drawn to their temple.

When I finished talking, she just kept looking at me, intensely, for a moment. And then she nodded and said firmly, in a British accent, "I like you. This will work out."

I was at this temple for a solid month. Caru and Vai, married 51 years now — he an American who protested and avoided the Vietnam War by traveling abroad, and she a fine artist from Great

Britain who met Caru during that time in Singapore — lived in a log cabin just past the bird aviary, second garden, and open-air llama barn. Vai painted in the garret, mostly stunning, colorful murals to be displayed in the temple, here as well as the one in Salt Lake City, both of which she designed. All her work was in service to the deity Krishna.

A large wing of that home had a separate entrance with an additional four bedrooms and bathroom, where visitors stayed. My first week there, it was just Radaka and me in our own rooms. Since it wasn't appropriate for a monk to be sharing a bathroom with a woman, he was able to use a spare bathroom in the main house, which meant I had the bathroom to myself.

We only crossed paths by the house each day when he was removing his orange clothing from drying on the fence, and I put my tank tops and farm pants on it after bucket-washing them, as we had no access to either a washing machine or dryer (but, as I told Vai when she passed and commented on how happy I looked, I was grateful to have readily-available water, which I wouldn't have had in the Peace Corps). I'd also often see Radaka in the temple when I would swing in daily to drop off the garden harvests. He always looked happy, too.

Twice a day I dipped into the outstanding vegetarian buffet — a veritable feast of six or so entrées and a colorful salad bar including three types of fruit (which had been particularly hard for me to get while traveling these past three months). These were the fruits of my labor here while WWOOFing.

Sundays at dinner were different, however. Called The Love Feast, and celebrated every Sunday evening at about 400 Hare Krishna temples around the world, it included a service with call-and-response chanting, dancing, and rituals like you might find in any church, and an inspiring talk like a sermon or homily, followed by all of us (a truly fascinating diversity of people, by the way) sitting down together outside afterwards to dine on the ever-changing spread of delectables.

Caru's talk that first Sunday was extraordinary — and highly timely for me. It was on distractions and reminded me that I don't need to choose my next step, at least not yet. My higher power has a destiny for me in mind, and all I need to do is continually hear and heed my calling. He said much more, and much more eloquently, but this is what I took away. From my seat way in the back, the lone masked person out of an abundance of caution when indoors while traveling, I nodded in understanding.

When I thanked him later for his words, he thanked *me*. He said he could tell I was engaged and that helped him as a speaker.

I realized we helped each other in ways we don't even know just by being. I knew, especially after these past three months traveling, that I was a positive, joy-based person who believed in what other people often consider to be impossible. Through my natural instinct to find creative solutions, I saw alternative realities and took concrete steps to bring them to, shall we say, fruition. I iterated over and over, continually asking *what if*.

I pilot tested. I experimented. I turned over every idea to see all its angles. I created safe spaces for magic. This was what I was best at. Bureaucratic institutions consider this to mean never being satisfied (in a bad way). Entrepreneurial organizations (such as many where I've worked) consider this my strength.

I realized as I danced while chanting "Hare Krishna, Hare Krishna, Hare Hare, Rama Rama" that any thoughts of running for mayor of my city were just a distraction from my purpose, of course. The amount of energy I would need to spend dealing with negative toxicity and a pervasive attitude of *can't* rather than *can* would be a distraction from my calling.

A new day would dawn for me, with renewed clarity. I would be needed elsewhere eventually. But for right then, I was needed right there, exactly where I was. Fully present. Without distractions. Irrigating. Tending. Weeding. Harvesting.

I needed to trust this abundant journey. Life was a buffet. A veritable love feast.

A few days later, Independence Day, I was eating outside at the wooden table on the veranda of the temple when Caru walked by with yet another baby bird. He'd been saving them after they blew out of their nests the night before during a truly violent "microburst" — a quick, intense storm with 70 miles/113 kilometers-per-hour winds that lasted at least 10 times longer than normal, per Caru's wife, Vai, and which I thought was going to blow llamas through my window. The winds caused me to crouch in the hallway with my bike helmet on and my to-go bag.

"How's it going with the birds?" I asked.

"Not so great, but I have to try," he replied.

He then wished me a happy July 4th. With our country in such turmoil, I said vaguely that there was always hope. I was simply grateful for the dozen or so peacocks on the property, which looked like little fireworks when they fanned their feathers — just as I was grateful for Lish's brightly-colored chicken eggs when I was at her goat farm in North Carolina on Easter.

Caru then said nonchalantly, "We can see the fireworks from Provo from the temple, you know."

The fireworks in Provo? My mother had been texting me about them. The Freedom Festival in Provo had been getting coverage on the news all day, she said. (The last two places I stayed, Salt Lake City and Boulder, both announced they were planning non-pyrotechnic drone-delivered displays due to wildfire risk. Even though I passed a Smokey the Bear billboard just down the road — I kid you not — the fireworks were still a *go* here.)

Caru then informed me there was a terrace around the entire top of the temple.

A terrace around the entire top? I'd been here for more than a week and I had yet to discover this?

I went up at sunset and circled it over and over again, each view of the sun and the mountains more beautiful than the one before it. This was the time of day when the peacocks all seemed to fan their feathers, and my mother enjoyed FaceTiming to see them, as well as the llamas laying amongst the sagebrush, faces turned toward the setting sun, and I was excited to call her and tell her about my discovery.

At 10:00 PM, per Caru's advice, I headed back to the temple and climbed the long outdoor staircase illuminated only by the light of my cell phone. The fireworks were already sounding and I hurried. No one else was there.

At the top, I turned toward Provo and I reveled in the full visibility of a line of vibrant bursts. And then I glanced sideways and gasped. Could it be? *Could it be?* Could there be fireworks in *all four direction*s, at the base of every single surrounding mountain?

I ran around the terrace, laughing, bats whirring around my head, the peacocks screaming from the noise in the distance.

I tried to call both my husband and mother again — they had to see this! — but my phone service was spotty and I couldn't connect. Instead, I told myself to be fully present. *We may never pass this way again.* I sat on the stairs and just enjoyed it all, the stars now registering in my vision as well. I had three family members currently struggling with eye problems and I didn't take this ability to see for granted. There might be a day I could no longer see. Today was not that day.

The bat sounds overwhelming, I headed back to my modest home, thoughts of marmots in my mind. I knew they lived under the shed, and I had even seen one of these large groundhog-like rodents earlier in the day. Were they nocturnal? Did they bite? Were they rabid? Did they have plague like the prairie dogs I saw in Colorado? I walked faster.

Luckily, I didn't see any, but I wondered what else didn't I see in life. What else was hiding in plain sight?

That week was very nice. Being the only WWOOFer there had its benefits. I enjoyed the solitude and working at my own pace, riding my bike, and taking llamas for walks at night. I also loved the direct access to both Vai and Caru. But the pace of growth of the yellow squash and zucchini was exceeding my ability to keep up with it while also eliminating squash bugs, pruning tomatoes, watering both gardens every day, and doing other chores to ensure a bountiful harvest.

I was grateful when Akash and Valeria arrived. Originally from India and Italy, they now lived in Berlin and had found this temple through a program similar to WWOOF called Workaway. They got the room across from me.

At about the same time, a devotee (which is what Krishna practitioners are called) named Parama arrived from India. He got Radaka's room, who then moved into the main part of the log cabin closer to his bathroom. Shortly thereafter, Fatima, originally from North Africa, arrived from Paris. She got the fourth and final room in our wing. And then 20-year-old Alva, the youngest of the bunch, arrived from Germany as well. She got another room in the main part of the log cabin — I never did find out how she and Radaka worked out the bathroom situation.

So we were filled up, spanning a 40-year age difference from Alva to me, and another 18 years if you counted Caru and Vai, and I loved them all. While squashing bugs and harvesting together, learning about each of their unique circumstances reminded me once again that there were so many ways to live a life, to build bridges across countries and generations, and to change courses (which they had all done in some way at some time) by pivoting rather than quitting.

Akesh and Valeria kicked off their time in the United States in a highly unusual way —pack-training llamas at this unique Krishna Temple in Mormon country.

Akash and I tried to hold Pada as the young brown llama bucked and kicked and twirled, not wanting to wear the pack on his back. These were large animals, twice the size of alpacas, and their force was clear when they wanted to show it.

We were training Pada and Puri, the two llamas I had been walking each evening on my own time so they would get used to trekking, as is their destiny here. But Pada wasn't feeling Zen about any of it.

Vai said it took one to three sessions until a llama gets comfortable with the pack on his back. He will be rented out. He will be expected to trek up to 10 miles/16 kilometers carrying up to 100 pounds/161 kilograms. That is how the male llamas earned their keep here, although Vai and Caru were shifting more to breeding, as they were getting older and the labor of renting the llamas out was getting to be too much.

Vai was good with the llamas. Great, actually. She was the mama llama. Still recovering from a recent life-threatening foot infection, which is why she had been limping, she mostly pointed her cane at us and told us what to do, and we tried.

But this time with Pada crossed my line. I was in over my head, and I knew it. I did not feel safe. As Vai was directing my next move, my hand gripping Pada's harness firmly, I replied adamantly, "I am at my limit."

Vai repeated the direction more calmly and coaxed me forward (and I know I was safe in her hands), but I had acknowledged my boundary — and if there's one thing I've learned on this trip, it's that I don't second-guess myself.

"I am at my limit," I stated again, more emphatically, and she saw the look on my face and understood. She quickly relieved me of the llama and Valeria took over. She then asked me to lead a tour, adding that I had gotten a five-star review for the tour I did the week before (my first llama tour ever). And so, I did.

Pack training would happen again each Saturday, but I was no longer a part of it. Vai had me lead tours on Saturdays instead. I was proud of myself for speaking up for my needs, and for being able to pivot.

After leading my first tour, by the way, I realized how much I didn't know and wanted to get more informed before the next one once I realized this was going to be my thing. I had been a tour guide with Bicycle Tours of Atlanta and took my responsibility very seriously to provide a quality experience for paying guests. I felt the same way here.

The morning of my next tour, I reviewed the pages of notes from my frantic online searches the night before. The history of the International Society of Krishna Consciousness. The size of the temple dome where I was currently WWOOFing. Facts about African Grey and Macaw parrots. Koi fish. Llamas. Peacocks.

None of that mattered.

What mattered that day was that Tyler used a wheelchair and could not get up the hill to the pond to see the koi, so I videotaped them and brought the fish to him and it made him smile.

What mattered was that the mom with the baby on her hip and a class of daycare kids with her didn't cut the apples they brought, and thus the kids couldn't feed the llamas — and I had a knife.

They giggled as the llama lips tickled their hands when they fed the cut apples to them.

What mattered was that even though I mistakenly chose a llama to showcase who is ornery, spits and doesn't like to be brushed (and got rammed by the lead male stud while I was standing there holding him for the group to see), a teenage boy who loves llamas, there with his sister and mom, was ecstatic just to spend time with them (the llamas, his family).

What mattered was actually quite simple — although I now know lots of fun facts. If you want to know what a baby llama is called, how long it takes peacocks to develop their tail feathers, or what koi are the symbol of in Japan, I'm your party guest.

However wonderful life at the temple was, it got even better when I rode my bike. Spanish Fork, Utah, turned out to be my favorite place to ride my bike on the entire journey — I even looked up homes for sale there — and I think it's all thanks to Joseph Smith, publisher of The Book of Mormon in 1830.

Bear with me because my Church of Latter Day Saints knowledge is limited to three things: the pioneer journals I bought at a thrift store on Main Street in Spanish Fork that sold what's referred to as Mormonabilia (I bought a mission journal written by a man named John C. Hall between 1852-1857); the patience of lapsed Mormons, now Krishna devotees, in answering my questions; and a series named *Hell on Wheels* that my husband and I watched and loved about the building of the first railroad across the United States in the late 1800s. But if my facts are right, Smith issued specific rules as to how Mormon cities should look and this included roads wide enough to turn a team of oxen.

This extra width now meant that Spanish Fork (and, I'm guessing, many cities in Utah) had enormous shoulders on its roads and I could ride my bike literally everywhere. Spanish Fork had also built some beautiful multi-use paths that went to a wide variety of destinations.

Every single day was a new adventure on my bike. I fell upon a brand new community garden; a business named Compassion Mobility that sold adaptive vans, bikes and ATVs for people with disabilities; a park named Adventure Heights that was designed to be inclusive to everyone; apricot trees hanging heavy with ripe fruit; and finally more wind turbines! I found them by chance after riding up a steep series of switchbacks (zigzags in a road or trail's construction that make it easier to climb a steep hill) on a path aptly named Dripping Rocks Trail, which had a caged area for falling boulders and had me holding my breath the entire way. I danced, of course.

I even discovered a food pantry named Tabitha's Way, where I volunteered one evening. It reminded of how much I enjoyed volunteering at Pete's food pantry garden in Boulder.

When I rode my bike to Provo (a total of 28 miles/45 kilometers in scorching heat), I visited Brigham Young University (a Silver-level Bicycle Friendly University with the League of American

Bicyclists, by the way, and up on a hill like the University of North Carolina in Chapel Hill). I met a young woman tending her garden outside her tiny home. I ate beignet-like things (I was getting closer!) called kolaches that come in both savory and sweet versions at a famous place named Hruska's, and then stopped at two community assistance places and a related community garden. They are everywhere in our communities, by the way, and they need our help. Even if it's just an hour, or even if you just drop some stuff off.

I couldn't stop thinking about the community garden I had helped start back at home 14 years ago. They were still doing great work and had continued their partnership with the food pantry, donating 20% of its produce to it, since the day we started that garden. All of the other founders had moved on — three of them had died — and I had not been involved with them for years because one of the new boards decided to lock the garden gate, thereby cutting off public access. This was against our values as founders, and I couldn't get off my high horse about it.

It was ironic to me that one of the very best examples, gate aside, of a nonprofit doing the kind of work I loved was just two miles from my home and I didn't feel at home there anymore. This had been weighing on me for years and made me feel bitter. I didn't want to feel that way anymore, but how? I didn't yet know a way to resolve this. But I would. One day, I would.

There had been so much laughter on this journey about things that happened every day that I know will make me smile the rest of my life. Perhaps those are the gifts I've given myself by taking this journey. Some funny things are hard to explain, the ways things are when you truly just had to be there. But as I passed an old broken-down barn on my way back to the Krishna temple from Spanish Fork each day, I kept laughing about something I want to share.

That barn reminded me of the old tobacco drying barn on Lish's goat farm in North Carolina. Thinking of Lish's repurposed tobacco farm reminded me of what happened there, followed by what happened half a country away a month later.

Lish had planted something called fenugreek from a bag of seeds she bought in the spice aisle of the supermarket, and it was growing super well when I was there. She gave me little baggies of it to plant across the USA when I left. We thought this would be fun. I remembered the baggies of fenugreek seeds one day at the communal lunch in Kansas when we were all discussing upcoming things we wanted or needed to do there on the farm. I said, "I have fenugreek to plant, if you have a good place for it." So far, so good, right?

Sister Imelda, the 85-year-old herbalist in this celibate sisterhood, wasn't familiar with it and asked, her interested piqued, "What is fenugreek good for?"

Seventy-eight-year-old Sister Jane was already searching online. Always good-humored, a smile crept up the edge of her lips when she read, "Fenugreek helps improve interest in sex."

A moment of silence followed.

Then Sister Imelda announced in a deadpan voice, "I don't think we need to prioritize the planting of that right now."

No. No, we do not. Not there.

Honestly, even writing this is making me laugh again.

But it gets better.

Moving on in the lunchtime conversation, others announced upcoming events, chores with which they needed help, and expected visitors. Then Sister Jane stated nonchalantly, "On Saturday, I'm participating in breeding."

Heads perked up, and someone had to say it. So I did.

"Then you're gonna need the fenugreek."

We laughed so hard. And you know what? I will be laughing about that forever.

Maybe you will, too, anytime you pass an innocent-looking broken-down barn in your travels or fenugreek seeds in the spice aisle. You may even decide to plant them.

I really wanted to pinch myself sometimes on this journey when I witnessed truly sustainable practices. It seemed lately like society was moving in the opposite direction, and these small glimpses gave me glimmers of hope.

While picking fruit up an apricot tree overlooking the koi pond in front of the Krishna temple, I reflected on the closed-loop growing methods in practice here. The peacocks worked alongside me in the upper garden when I weeded, harvested beets, picked lower leaves and what's called suckers off tomato plants, hilled up potatoes, and watered from the fish-fertilized pond. They were eating bugs.

The bats that lived in the two rear domes on top of the Krishna temple joined them in this Sisyphean chore at night. The llamas contributed their manure to the growing of food on the acre in cultivation here, split between that garden next to the temple and the larger one down below the temple.

Volunteers — both regular and random — came and went, and they were all a joy to chat with while working. Some had never seen an eggplant or pepper plant before in their lives. Some grew up with gardens and felt like they were coming home again when they dug their hands in the soil.

Vai weighed in continually, her knowledge of this land and its habits and needs essential, always willing to let go and trust that whatever happens is Krishna's will. She insisted that first-harvests of any new crop be offered to Krishna at the altar first, and that the souls of pulled weeds be blessed as we released them from their Earth-based home. This resulted in intentional moments where we truly honored what we were doing, which was a nice reminder of the miracles in front of me each day.

We came from all walks of life. All beliefs. All species. And we worked together out there in the garden — and increasingly in our hearts. As I told a large volunteer group from a correctional facility that I was leading one Saturday morning (in lieu of pack-llama training), "The hands before us have prepared and planted this land and it's our job now to just hold it up and carry its intentions to the next group of hands. The most important thing I want you to know today is that you are necessary."

I thought of my sweatshirt and added, "The world is a better place with you in it, and you are enough." For the next two hours, I had never seen a group of twenty people work harder.

That was how a garden, and a world, could grow. If that's cult-like, I can think of worse.

What *was* worse was the weather. Almost every day was now habitually over 100 degrees Fahrenheit/38 degrees Celsius. As a result, I had shifted my work hours so that I was in the gardens from six to 10 in the morning, Brad's sun hat my most prize possession more than ever along with my long-sleeved shirt, pants and zinc sunblock.

My bike rides got shorter, but since it was, indeed, a dry heat (as they say about the heat out West), as opposed to the stifling humidity of Georgia, I actually still enjoyed them. Frequent stops at a local spot named Glade's for an ice cream cone at the walk-up window helped, as did leisurely hangs along Spanish Fork Creek in my hammock and easy access to public water fountains, where I refilled my water bottles constantly. I was increasingly concerned, however, about my next WWOOF workstay.

I knew planning a stop in the Mojave Desert in late July/early August was risky, however interesting the aquaponics eco-farm sounded. Can you say hottest days on Earth in the hottest *place* on Earth? That's where I was going next, and this year's temperatures were more extreme than ever. When you find yourself searching at what temperature do contact lenses adhere to eyeballs, it's time to rethink the plan.

To be fair, the desert location where I was going was entirely off the grid, so electricity would not have been an issue. But water and food and the swamp cooler's ability to maintain a temperature compatible with human life would have been (or at least I was never fully assured that it wouldn't be).

What's more, the desert eco-farm hadn't had any reviews since 2018 (lack of reviews, such as Candida's horse sanctuary, or a long time since a review, is a red flag, I'd learned). The farm's remote location an hour away from the nearest big city (Las Vegas) would require me to rely on my point person, who no longer lived on the farm (or, as best as I can tell, even went there daily). And trucks that break down in deserts equal death. It was spitting distance (so to speak, channeling my llama-spitting experience) until I turned 60 years old, by the way, and I wanted to reach that age, thank you very much.

So I changed my plans, due to climate, securing a longer stay at the WWOOF location I had scheduled for after the Mojave Desert farm in the High Desert of California. Climate changes in our plans are nothing new, of course. We've always had to contend with rained-out picnics or snow days from school changing our plans. It is just that the stakes keep getting higher, and the news keeps getting more dire. Europe. India. Africa. Alaska. Vermont. The Southwestern United States. Everywhere.

It was the right decision, but I was still sad about it. My contact, a Primary Care Physician who practiced and lived about an hour away from the farm, had been nice. He was excited to share the experiments they were doing and even supplied me with a 90-page document about their eco-farm. But my gut said no, and I trusted it. It was really that simple.

I decided to still spend a night in Vegas on my way to California since the bus went that way anyway, and I was curious what 115 degrees Fahrenheit/44 degrees Celsius would feel like. Plus, let's face it, that night in the king suite on The Strip (which I got for a very affordable rate) would feel like I won the jackpot after these past four months, which, may I remind you, had included bucket laundry washing, cold showers, sleeping on buses, digging holes to defecate, and refusing to stay at one place because of a rodent infestation. What's a little heat when you have glitz?

In addition to the final WWOOF stay, California would mean seeing my family again and the ceremonial dipping of my bike tire in the Pacific Ocean. Even though I'd been traveling between major cities via buses and trains, I'd already logged over 1,000 miles/1,609 kilometers on my little trusty folding bike during this trip.

My journey home would then consist of a three-day swoop through the hot-as-Hades American Southwest via train (with no sleepette reserved) and an early-morning view of the Superdome in New Orleans on the mournful anniversary of Hurricane Katrina. Plus, if there was still a God (or Krishna), *beignets*.

With a little Vegas luck on my side, the USA passenger rail system would finally deliver me back home to Atlanta, Georgia — where hubby, by the way, had been doing an astounding job keeping the ol' homestead afloat. He was even out there with the clippers on almost a daily basis and had, I believe, a new understanding of what I had been doing out there on the property we've been stewarding all these years.

It blew my mind to be able to visualize the rest of this journey *actually happening*, and I was starting to look forward to being home for a change. After helping grow so many other people's farms and gardens across the USA, I wanted to plant my own again. It was getting near the time to put down some roots.

But first, it was time for Akesh and Valeria to leave. They said they were leaving at 7:00 AM but when I took a break from the upper garden to look for them at that time, they were already gone. Someone told me they left earlier to be sure not to miss the bus.

The bus stop was about a half mile away, and it was already approaching 100 degrees Fahrenheit/38 degrees Celsius. I grabbed a few water bottles just in case they needed them, hopped on my bike, and whipped down the hill. I had to say goodbye to them and make sure they got off okay, especially knowing how many bus problems I had experienced already on this journey. They smiled when they saw me approaching and were grateful for the extra waters.

I watched them board the bus and head on to the rest of their lives after our serendipitous two-week overlap. *We may never pass this way again.* But would I ever see Valeria and Akesh again somewhere else in this suddenly-smaller world? I wondered this about everyone I met. Life had a funny way of turning out. There were really no coincidences. Everyone I met I was meant to meet, for reasons none of us may ever know. This was an absolutely lovely couple who both made me laugh out loud, and I missed them immediately.

Next, it was my turn to leave. After everyone at the Krishna Temple signed my duck hat, I packed my bags and twirled in the doorway to Willie Nelson as the llamas and peacocks watched me. I had a final lunch at the vegetarian buffet (my 60th meal there), and then headed out on my bike on the road again to that same bus stop where Valeria and Akesh had departed a few days earlier.

It was Pioneer Day, a state holiday that commemorates the entry of Brigham Young and the first Mormons to the territory of Utah. The local 822 bus wasn't running in the morning due to a parade in Spanish Fork, which was part of a larger celebration called Fiesta Days. Fiesta Days included a rodeo (where I strolled around unencumbered during daytime practice sessions, invisible aging woman that I am), a street festival (which was similar to my city's Lemonade Days, which was started after our devastating tornado to raise money to replant our suburban forest) and the Cowboy Church event I attended.

At Cowboy Church, by the way, I had parked my bike in the back of the room and was leaning against a wall eating a donut and fruit from the lovely hospitality table when the cowboy-in-charge came up to me and asked if that was my bike.

I replied, "No, that's my *horse*."

He smiled broadly and put up his fist for a bump and exclaimed, "Welcome, Cowgirl!"

So you can just call me Cowgirl from now on, thank you very much.

One thing became abundantly clear to me: Hare Krishna, Hare Krishna; what a friend we have in Jesus. It's all just *trust the journey* in one way or another.

By the way, I had been in no rush to leave Spanish Fork that day. I was heading to a basic hotel in Provo so that I would be where I needed to be, no stress, for my morning bus to Vegas. I had learned, budget aside, that these kinds of precautions were necessary considering the propensity for bus *issues*. If you are planning a journey like this in the United States, you need more money in your transportation budget than you think — if I haven't already made that clear!

So with this local bus delay on my hands, I decided to first ride my bike to the parade. The business that I loved so much that sold adaptive vans, bikes and ATVs had crowned a woman who uses a wheelchair as Miss Compassion Mobility. She rode on a colorful float, clearly made with love and joy, alongside Miss Utah County and Miss Teen Utah.

I met them all at the parade when the social media manager remembered me from when I met her at the store, and she flagged me over. I took photos of the three women, all appearing to be enjoying their exciting day. An announcement shortly after the parade named Compassion Mobility as the winner of the Mayor's Choice Award. That gave me hope for an increasingly inclusive society.

And yet, there I was the next morning, sitting on a curb in Provo in the heat waiting for the bus and peeing. This was hard enough being able-bodied. What happens when I no longer am? What about those who currently aren't?

# 7

## Hot Streak

A coach bus rounded the corner and I started to gather my things.

"Vegas?" I asked the bus driver, rhetorically to just confirm.

He replied, "No. Salt Lake City. Yours is next."

*Please arrive; please arrive,* I felt my brain repeating as I waited the extra minutes.

And then it did.

But it wasn't a bus. It was a 17-person van, with a pull-along trailer behind it for luggage — and my bike.

Confirming the inclusion of my bike on this trip had been difficult and had, in fact, consumed several hours of my time a week before. I had booked the trip through the USA's main bus company and I saw that they had contracted with this local partner. I looked up the local company and discovered happily that they espoused their bike-friendliness. Their online information said I needed to let them know I had a bike just a day before.

Out of an abundance of caution, however, I called the week before. The agent on the phone told me that since I booked it through the main bus company, I needed to confirm the bike through them, that they had an additional charge for it. I told them that the main bus company typically had a place online where I could check a box indicating that I had a bike but they didn't for this route. Hence, why I was calling.

No good. They said I had to call that company, which I did. That company's agent told me that I had to go to the main bus company's office the morning of my trip and get my bike bag weighed in order to determine if there was a charge and what it would be (since it was calculated by weight). This was a logistics complication that I knew had the potential to derail me yet again — the bus station didn't open until timing would already be tight for my local provider's curbside bus — so I called the local provider back.

I had decided I would make my reservation directly through the local provider and cancel the main bus company's reservation. I hated canceling them because they do not give you a refund — they only give you credit toward a future ride, and I had already accumulated more than enough of that during my journey.

When I went to book my trip through the local provider, I told the agent what had transpired. She agreed this was ridiculous and told me she was going to find a better solution. Miracle of miracles, she actually called me back.

"I kept your reservation with the main bus company but found a way to book the bike through us. It costs 10 dollars, and you can simply give that in cash to the driver."

A kind, competent customer service agent who actually solved the problem! Hope, once again, prevails.

I nabbed the door spot on the van, even though that meant people had to continually crawl over me to get on and off. There was really no COVID-safe spot since we were pretty scrunched together, but at least I could look out the window (masked).

I was in for a treat. From the Colorado Plateau to the Mojave Desert, the Virgin River had carved out a gorge of cliffs and canyons that included both Zion National Park in southern Utah and Lake Mead in Nevada. The highway we were on, I-15, was apparently one of the most expensive expanses of highway ever built due to the diverse terrain topography. Short answer? Breathtaking. My smallness was accentuated even more so in that van instead of a bus.

While walking back to the van at a gas station after using the restroom, a man by a motorcycle asked where my bike was, pointing to my bike helmet hanging from my arm.

"On the van," I answered, pointing to it.

"Oh, I thought for a second you had a motorcycle, too," he replied.

We got to chatting pleasantly. He was another Vietnam Veteran (I wondered how Mike was doing) and was on his way to do a ride with some childhood friends of his. One of his friends was experiencing early dementia and they all knew this would be his last ride. It was touching and I enjoyed talking with him.

No part of me flirts with guys, ever, and I did not do so here. I'd like to make that abundantly clear before I tell you what happened next. Reminder that this book is not Eat Pray Love. It's more Eat Pray Quack (or even Eat Pray Llama).

*He asked me to join him.*

That was of course a big, fat and immediate no.

Back in the van with no regrets, I watched him pull away and realized, in an alternate reality, I could be on my way to who knows where on the back of a motorcycle. I could be painting bikes in New York City; greeting guests at the hotel in Joplin; herding alpacas in Pawnee Rock, Kansas; and riding my bike around Spanish Fork, Utah. I had even passed an Airstream camper for sale in Salem, Utah, and had lingered on the road by it for way too long, just imagining. *There are so many ways to live a life.* Would I go back to the life I left, or would I change it as a result of this journey?

My sliding doors moment done, I settled in as the van got on its way. We passed energy facilities, which I found fascinating, and a sign welcoming us to Arizona, which was a surprise to me because I didn't know I was going to Arizona! Turns out we just nipped the corner of it.

Back in Nevada, the desert rolled out in front of us, Momma's Amazing Adventure playlist in my ears: *One day you will reach the desert.* I made it. *I made it.* I thought of quitting so many times, maybe even every single day, and here I was. In the Mojave Desert. I honestly could not believe it.

About an hour outside Vegas, the man behind me in the van shouted that the driver had missed a stop. It had been almost an hour ago. *You're shit outta luck*, I almost said out loud, remembering how I stood there waving my arms in Ellis, Kansas and the bus driver just kept going.

But then the driver got off the highway — and turned around!

The van fell silent.

Two babies in the row in front of me started to fuss at exactly the same time and a quick-acting mom pulled out a device and popped on a children's video. A song lyric filled the van. It was, unfortunately, this one:

*If you're happy and you know it, clap your hands.*

No one clapped.

Instead, I could almost hear everyone mentally calculating how the time delay would impact them. I didn't blame them. Everyone had somewhere to be. Time is precious. That two-hour detour (one hour back, one hour back on track) cost folks.

I had no one waiting for me in Vegas. No dinner plans. No show to catch. But time was ticking for me as well. My 60th birthday was less than a month away now. I kept thinking about how you think you get 80 years, but COVID, constant news of suicides, and my recent pre-cancerous diagnosis reminded me that wasn't the case.

I tried to be, fully *be*, wherever I was, and in just a few more minutes that would mean standing in a parking lot in 111 degrees Fahrenheit/44 degrees Celsius waiting for a rideshare. You will be happy to know that my research — and lived experience — revealed that contact lenses do not melt until a much, much higher temperature. My shoes, however, were another story but that wasn't until 114 degrees Fahrenheit/45 degrees Celsius the next day.

An Eastern European immigrant named Maverick picked me up at 3:06 PM Pacific Time. *Pacific Time.* I was now on Pacific Time! *One day you will see the ocean,* that song on Momma's Adventure Playlist continued. The ocean was still a few weeks away for me, but it was now within striking distance. I was *in the zone.*

He was chatty and I treasured hearing about his journey to America and his time in Vegas. All around us, construction for the Grand Prize Formula 1 Race in November was underway. It was being touted as the biggest sporting event in Vegas history. The Sphere, a dome-shaped concert and entertainment venue, had just finished construction as well. Things were happening.

Maverick dropped me at the fancy hotel and wished me well. His soft eyes and kind smile had meant a lot to me. I snapped open my bike, strapped on my things and walked through the automatic doors to the grand lobby. I was hot and smelly and most likely had hard-to-remove dirt still embedded in my nails from the gardens and llamas. My sun hat from Brad hung off my backpack and my sleeping bag and travel pillow knocked against my sides in their little duffles.

I stood on line along with the other guests, their fancy bags and pretty clothes a contrast. I was a long way from "Welcome, Cowgirl!"

The desk clerk, however, welcomed me as warmly as anyone else and gave me the key to my suite. I paraded my motley self through the casino to the elevators, stopping to record a quick video, slot machines behind me, to let folks know I had made it to Vegas.

I dropped my bags in my luxurious room; peed in the gold-accented bathroom; splashed some water on my dirty face and yes, Tom, even brushed my hair. I then headed back down to explore. I knew from previous research I had done that many of the hotels in Vegas were doing some wonderful things relating to all aspects of triple-bottom-line sustainability, and the Venetian's website had not disappointed with details. I set out to find them.

I grabbed a green smoothie and strolled around the enormous hotel, eventually falling upon the fake canal with the gondolas. A Vegas classic. A must-do, or so the advertisement for it said. The line to ride wrapped around this artificial mall-like space, and a sign said only indoor rides were available due to the heat. *No, thank you.* I kept walking.

I wandered into the casino and asked the guy at the guest relations desk a simple question, or so I thought, and it wasn't about hope.

"How do you gamble?" I asked. I don't like casinos but my dad had asked me to play a dollar for him.

"Excuse me?" He answered, leaning closer. Maybe I was muffled because of my mask.

"How do you gamble?" I replied. "I've never been here."

"Ohhhhh, " he said, getting animated, "Well, if you use this card and you do this and that, you get points and you can redeem for food and stays and if this and that and then and. . . . ."

*Whoa; hold your horses.* He had lost me.

I rephrased my question.

"I mean, more basically, can I just put a dollar in the machine?"

He laughed and said, "Yes. Yes, just slip it in."

So I approached a noisy, flashing machine and tried to figure it out before putting the dollar in. It was so chaotic. I moved to another one and another and another, all of them bombarding my senses, confusing me, unnerving me. I hated it. I hated it and I knew I needed to get out.

I walked out onto The Strip, where blasts of heat smacked me in the face. It was stifling. Even dry heat apparently has a level where it exceeds livability. I strolled just a block or so through this Disney-World-for-Adults before heading back to the hotel.

As I was about to enter, I saw my reflection in the door and told myself, "Okay. Now let's do it *your* way."

Once I made this my focus, I quickly discovered a plaque indicating the hotel was LEED (Leadership in Energy and

Environmental Design)-certified at the Gold level; a sign in the bathroom stating how the Venetian is committed to social responsibility and the elimination of human trafficking and what to do if you were a victim of it or saw suspicious activity; recycling bins, lots of healthy food choices, water conservation practices, and participation in the Chefs to End Hunger program. This was a regional non-profit organization that distributed leftover meals to local charities. I finally felt at home. Aren't *I* a barrel of monkeys?

The next morning, I intended to do a little early-morning bike ride on The Strip before all the motor vehicles and crushing heat, but then when I walked into my grand bathroom and saw the sparkling tub, I pivoted. I didn't need another moment out there in Vegas.

I drew a bath instead. I drew a breath. And I drew a circle around myself as a cocoon from the heat and noise and constant bombardment of bad news. I pampered this road-strengthened, farm-chiseled, almost-60-year-old vessel of a body with which I've been entrusted for just a brief time here on Earth. And it was glorious.

They say what happens in Vegas stays in Vegas. But I will tell you this — the biggest gamble I've taken in life never happened on a casino floor. It happened when I chose to continue to hope for a better tomorrow. And that is something I pray — Hare Krishna, Hare Krishna, what a friend we have in Jesus, trust the journey — goes far beyond Vegas.

*Squish, Squish. Squish.* I could feel the soles of my shoes melting as I walked to my bus stop. As news reports from that time indicate, the shoes of a crossing guard in Arizona and a woman in Colorado melted as well. In fact, many people were reporting their shoes melting. This was another side effect from climate change, and I experienced it literally right where the rubber hit the road.

I also got a headache and felt dizzy, both symptoms I attributed to the 114-degree heat. I knew that people were getting burned when falling during this heat wave so I tried to walk extra slowly, but still fast enough that I would make it there before my shoes melted through. How's that for a fun little party game?

I passed a rainbow staircase along the way that was like the one I had danced up in Salt Lake City. I paused a moment and considered it but it was just too hot to dance, which was a first for me on this journey.

I waited for my final bus of the journey, a big, white unmarked one like the first bus from Atlanta to Durham, and was grateful there was at least a portable tent set up over the stop. I joined the moms and children waiting underneath it, all of us looking like hell. There was just one small bench, already taken. No water. No bathroom. No food. We were on our way to Death Valley, and I wondered, perhaps, if we were already there.

And then it happened. I was assigned the number one seat you don't want on a bus — the one next to the number *two*. Welcome to my own little Death Valley. I survived everything else to date, but could I survive hours on this bus across the hottest place on Earth in The Toilet Seat?

Short answer? Masks! I'll never know if they kept me from catching COVID these past three years and throughout this journey or just muffled my voice in the casino, but that day they saved my life, or at least being able to breathe without smelling poop.

Rolling port-a-potty aside, I adored the Mojave National Preserve and its starker neighbor, the until-then dreaded Death Valley, which shocked me with its beauty. I buddied up with my seat mate and the two of us were glued to her window the entire way, with me leaning over to film things like one of the largest solar power facilities in the world.

I estimated loosely where the desert eco-farm was and knew I had made the right decision canceling that WWOOF workstay. As we passed random art and interesting cacti, however, I found myself longing to come back in an RV, one of those converted school buses called schoolies, or maybe that Airstream for sale in Utah to be able to stop and spend more time. Just not in this heat.

We were able to get out of the bus in Barstow, California — California! — for a fresh air break, and even though there was nothing fresh about the stiflingly hot air, I once again danced, all alone by a Route 66 sign. There would be one more Route 66 sign to come on my journey, but that one would boast a line of people waiting to commemorate their moment by it. To have this one all to myself, like the one in Joplin, felt decadent. I was so rich.

Many little moments on my journey felt predictably important but many more caught me off guard. The hellos and goodbyes on those train platforms from Durham to Philly. Vai in her studio in the mornings working on her peacock paintings, the sun streaming in. And now, tomatoes on the windowsill in my older daughter and fiancé's apartment in Los Angeles.

I had arrived at the bus parking lot across from Union Station in Downtown Los Angeles the night before, canceled that rideshare driver (a mutual decision) when he arrived with a full trunk, and taken two local trains. My future son-in-law, of course, offered to pick me up, but the traffic was so snarled that trains were really the best option. Plus, I had never ridden the trains in Los Angeles, and now I have.

As I was settling in at their apartment, I noticed the tomatoes and got suddenly teary. She was a grown-up now, with her own ripening tomatoes, her own ripening life. We had lined our sill with tomatoes while she was a child, when our garden was abundant and we also picked up CSA boxes weekly. We frequently named the tomatoes so my daughters could learn new things. The names of the planets. The Yankees line-up. Supreme Court justices. "When I was growing up, we had pizza with Justice Sotomoyor and Derek Jeter" is a true statement my daughters can make.

In addition to one of the best meals of my journey (that watermelon gazpacho was the perfect antidote to the desert heat), my daughter created a walking tour for us of Little Free Libraries and local shops. When we stopped at the local book store, I thought back to that book club meeting at my friend Judy's home in Chapel Hill. Would I one day have an author event here in Los Angeles? Would I one day look out and see my daughter's proud eyes upon me?

I know my daughters are watching me and I feel such a deep responsibility to lead by example, constantly defining and redefining what it means to be an aging woman in our country. At the end of the day, all I really want is to live my life until the last note of its song and to be a rock, a boulder, beneath their feet.

After two nights (with a scheduled return to my daughter in three weeks), I was on my way to what's called the High Desert of California, just an hour north of Los Angeles from Union Station via a comfortable commuter train. I was heading to my next and final WWOOF workstay — the one that would make my aspirational obituary true.

# 8

## La La Land

"She lived on a llama and lavender farm," it started. I deleted that and rewrote it several times. The same eight words. Deleted. Rewrote. Deleted. Rewrote.

It made no sense. How was I ever going to live on a llama and lavender farm?

I was off to a bad start with this assignment. When I was about to turn 40, it had been suggested to me that I write what's called an "aspirational obituary." This is when you imagine a look back at your life from the future; commit the dreams you have for your life to paper; and then perhaps see what parts of it you can actually make come true in the precious, unrepeatable resource of time you have left on this Earth.

Despite its improbability, I kept that first line in the obituary. Over the years, I would occasionally search "llama and lavender farm" on my computer and would come up empty-handed. These two things didn't seem to exist together anywhere on Earth. I increasingly did not see myself starting and running a farm in order to make this prediction true. So how would my obituary come to life?

Trust the journey, right? That seemed to be a big ask on this issue. And then, *Round America with a Duck* happened.

When I was researching for my cross-country experiential journey, I strung together my route serendipitously with just two mandatories: I needed to be in New York for my Dad's 90th birthday in April, and I needed to be in Los Angeles near the third week of August for my 60th birthday (my older daughter's bridal shower got planned and added later). Throw in the laborious back-and-forth messages with farmers trying to find the right fits and availabilities, cross-referenced with train and bus route schedules and fares, and it was a seemingly impossible puzzle.

It came together somewhat miraculously, however, except for that one last place. The farmer at the pomegranate, olive and grape vineyard, where I hoped to WWOOF in the Los Angeles area, replied that he was setting off on his own big adventure, so a potential farm workstay was out of the question. This disappointed me because it was just four miles/six kilometers from where my daughter's future in-laws lived. I hadn't met them in person yet and thought it would be a good opportunity to get to know them casually and comfortably during my off-time. I reached out to several other farmers in the LA area. No, no, no, and no. I was leaving home soon and this still wasn't locked in. Stress was mounting.

I tapped back into the WWOOF USA website and continued searching.

And then, there it was.

*Llama ranch and lavender farm nestled in the hills outside LA.*

My dream existed. It took 20 years for us to find each other. And now, I was living there. Just for a total of three weeks, but that counted. The impossible was possible. It was truly La La Land.

Now about to start the winter of my life (despite it still being the heat of summer), it was time to aspire to a new obituary, however morbid that sounded at first. An aspirational obituary wasn't about dying. It was about intentionally living your very best, most authentic life. It was never too early — or too late — to think about that.

I'm keeping that first line when I finally get around to writing the new obituary.

*She lived on a llama and lavender farm.*

Yes. Yes, I did.

Now, I wondered what other impossible things I could manifest, realizing that the start of my life's winter is not a darkness but, like the Winter Solstice, a return to the light.

What can *you* imagine into reality for your own life? Write it down. Say it out loud. The world conspires in your favor when you dare to dream.

It did for me.

Isolated on 250 acres/101 hectares just outside Agua Dulce, California, I was able to cobble together just a two-to-four-mile bike ride each day. It was the only bike riding I got to do during the three weeks I was at Long Look Ranch because the closest road had fast-moving motor vehicle traffic and no shoulders — where was Joseph Smith and his team of oxen when I needed them?

I had done just small rides at the goat farm in North Carolina, and I could do that again here. I knew that. After Boulder and Spanish Fork, however, I had gotten used to much longer rides that took me many new and exciting places, so it was a bit of an adjustment. *Be fully present*, I reminded myself. *We may never pass this way again.*

I started at the lower llama herd, passed the lavender fields where I harvested daily and then the old white adobe jail, complete with boarded up windows and an old door with bars on it, inside which I hung the fresh lavender to dry. I turned onto the next winding dirt road (like Kansas!) which had an old gold or borax mine and gorgeous views. I stopped to dance in the mine, and then I ascended even farther to the higher llama herd, chickens, pigs and a horse.

As I swept back downhill, I passed a stand of olive trees hanging heavy with their small green fruit, not yet ripe. One day while doing this loop, I snapped a photo. "Olive you!" I texted my husband. I even showed them to my mother during one of our evening video calls.

I dodged rattlesnakes, kept an eye out for coyotes and mountain lions, and learned the names of so much vegetation I had never seen before — California buckwheat, coastal pricklypear, thick-leaf Yerba Santa, tumbleweed — thanks to an app that Caru had recommended at the Krishna Temple in Utah when Vai asked me to identify the plants surrounding the koi pond. I was able to fulfill my assigned chore by using the app's one-week-free offer.

During that week, I also identified all the plants I had been passing every day on my long rides in wonderful Spanish Fork — things like rubber rabbitbrush, Scotch thistle, and that giant dandelion-like puff of wishes named yellow salsify.

I deleted the app when the free week trial was up and immediately regretted it. *What is this? What is that?* I kept saying out loud while passing flora new to me (or rather, now old friends but whose names I didn't know). I hoped perhaps the app would send me a special offer to lower the $30 annual charge, since I was on such a crazy tight budget during my journey and justifying that amount was a big ask.

No offer came. And now that I was in a brand new ecosystem for the first time in my life, wondering, wondering, wondering what everything was that I was passing on my bike each day, I bit the bullet and signed up.

Now I knew what those large grapefruit-like orbs were (pomelos). And those beautiful lily-like white flowers (sacred datura -- very poisonous). And the red berry-like dangles from trees (California peppertree). And chaparral yucca (which takes five to 10 years to reach maturity), Shaw's agave (apparently extremely endangered), and more.

The only thing that made me prickly was that I didn't sign up months earlier.

Between that app, exploring, visiting the animals, writing, dancing, staying in touch with friends and family and making TikToks, I was never bored or lonely during my free time, even without what I expected from the ranch's WWOOF profile to be daily relaxation at the above-ground pool (which was so mucky I was not going to step one foot near it — no need dying from a brain-eating amoeba at this point). In fact, I wouldn't have minded being the only WWOOFer there my entire time rather than just the first week, but then I would have missed Sarah (who was a returning WWOOFer there, having been gone just for my first week).

Sarah was my California-version of Laure (my apartment mate in Boulder), even similarly close in age to me (Sarah a few years younger, Laure a few years older). As with Laure, Sarah and I clicked immediately. I had, in fact, talked with her on the phone when she was at the ranch before I arrived because I wanted to make sure the living conditions met basic hygiene standards after the Missouri situation.

We shared a lovely renovated mobile home together (a big step-up from The Tin Can in North Carolina and especially that rodent-infested camper in Missouri). Its only quirk was that we had to turn a well on for about two hours every couple of days in order to fill up our water supply.

Turning the well on was hard and involved the very real possibility of encountering scorpions. *Scorpions.* Josette, the farm manager (who had kindly picked me up at the commuter train station in Santa Clarita), had caught one and put it in a glass jar to show me when I arrived.

It was also easy to forget to turn the water off, or to not do it all the way. I learned this the hard way. After Josette gave me a tour of the ranch and outlined the chores on the Friday I arrived, she then made it clear she was off on weekends. The ranch owners, Sheila and William, lived in a large house on a nearby road not on the ranch property and had texted to welcome me but made it pretty obvious that their life and mine would be separate. They had other jobs — he a property manager for film locations and an actor (although both the writers and actors guilds were currently on strike), and she a lawyer (and yet another US Navy Veteran).

Since the very ranch where I was WWOOFing was available as a film location, I would have liked to have seen this in action with crews and actors. As its Facebook listing reads: *Scroll through* to see Long Look Ranch, appropriately named for its hilltop views. Featuring outdoor seating, farm pens, chicken coop, outdoor pizza oven and fireplace, winding dirt roads, and much more — it's a charming Southwestern daydream. Plenty of space for base camp and crew parking. 100 acres located within the zone.

After so much time with so many people, either together at Love Feasts or "alone together" on buses and trains, I enjoyed my solitude that weekend. I loved catching up on writing, exploring, and laundry — I had both a washer and a dryer! I even cooked meals for the week with the generous bounty Josette had bought based on a detailed list I provided, honed from my lived experience across the country.

Monday morning came and I met Josette at 8:00 AM for our five hours of work (we soon shifted to earlier hours due to the heat). She asked how my weekend was and I briefed her on the good things that had happened. I then added, "The freshwater spring is pretty."

"The freshwater spring?" Josette replied quizzically. "We don't *have* a freshwater spring."

"The one coming down from the mountain," I answered. It had reminded me of the book and movie *Tuck Everlasting* all weekend.

Josette cocked her head and we both just looked at each other, not sure how two opposing statements could both be true. I then motioned for her to follow me and walked around the back of the mobile home to show her.

And there it was. The freshwater spring. Or rather, if you looked farther up the mountain, the overflowing well.

Ouch. My bad. Making sure that well was turned off all the way with its difficult-to-turn handle ended up being one of the harder physical tasks during this entire journey. (Loading the ATV with the enormous hay bales, at least four times as heavy as the bales in Kansas, was a close second.)

Later that week, I finally got to ride a horse. Thankfully, she was like that old horse Rooster I used to love riding back in Atlanta when I was in my 20s. Her name was Caroline and she had the same reddish brown coloring as the hair of that lovely college student, also named Caroline, with whom I WWOOFed in Kansas.

I missed Caroline-the-student a lot and wondered how her summer internship was going. She liked a lot of my posts on Instagram, but, as with a lot of young people, her social media feed was private. I didn't request access because these young folks didn't need some lady their mothers' age in their private spheres — I knew enough to respect that. I was just grateful to see she was still in mine, and feeling more hopeful about the world knowing every single young person I met was working in some field to improve it.

Josette had told me that WWOOFers here at Long Look Ranch got to help groom Caroline each Wednesday with a woman named Linda, so I did. Plus, we then took her for a long walk down the dirt road past the gold mine, me up in the saddle, Linda walking and jogging nearby and chatting. It was getting political in a way that felt unwelcome to me and I didn't want to go down that path so I just nodded occasionally and stroked Caroline's mane. It was so calming, like my own little hippotherapy session.

As Caroline bobbed gently in this beautiful arid High Desert, I let Linda's voice drift into the distance. I thought about being on a high horse about my morals sometimes and how that keeps me from participating in certain group things, like the community garden back in my Metro Atlanta city because of the locked gate. I wondered if there was a way I could honor my morals and get off my high horse at the same time. Was that even possible?

What about all the divides in our country, including the divide right here between Linda and me?

I tuned back in. I asked questions. *I listened.* I tried to see life from her perspective. My understanding had already shifted as I moved across the country, as I saw how harsh the landscapes were and how people treasured their independence. I took a moment to again see both the art (I filmed a stunning TikTok from the saddle of that horse) and cultural anthropology of the moment.

My second week there, Sarah returned and another WWOOFer, a recent college graduate named Andrew, arrived. He stayed in a really cute RV, which I almost asked to be switched to after he left but the bathroom situation there seemed questionable, and frankly,

I was pretty done with dealing with that by this point. I just needed to keep the well water flowing (not overflowing) and not get stung by a scorpion in the mobile home.

With Sarah knowing the ropes from her previous stay and me trained in the care and feeding of my third and fourth herds of camelids during this journey, Josette went on vacation for a week. Sarah, Andrew and I fell into a really nice routine. I did the animal chores in the morning, and Sarah and Andrew did them at night. Josette left a list of other tasks that we worked our way through as well. It was downright idyllic. We even all went into the gold mine many scary steps deeper than when I had gone alone, plus up to the top of a hill past mountain lion scat.

Before she left, I had asked Josette what one thing would make her day if she came back and it was done. She pointed to one of the large, caged overgrown garden beds.

"If that were cleaned out," she stated emphatically.

Sarah, Andrew and I ended up cleaning out *all* of them while Josette was gone. I climbed into each one and pulled massive amounts of weeds while Sarah pulled them around all the edges of the garden. Andrew loaded up the back of the ATV, and then drove it down the dirt road past the gold mine to the side path where green waste got left to compost. We did it all and were so proud of ourselves.

I had been scared to drive the ATV when I first arrived, by the way, but then I remembered the tractor in North Carolina and how that had made me nervous, too. *I can do this*, I told myself. Josette had cheered me on. This journey kept circling back on itself. And that was something to smile about.

Did someone say Smiley? My story was about to go full circle, yet again.

By my third and final week in the High Desert, it was starting to get cold at night. Not at first, when it was still roasting hot from the day and I was downing coconut waters to replace electrolytes, but suddenly in the middle of the night, after the rodents in the walls (and thankfully not in the house or anywhere near the utensil drawer!) had quieted down, but before the coyotes under the mobile home scurried back up the mountain.

I was waking up shivering, my nose ice cold. I discovered a space heater way off in the corner of my bedroom and used it to warm my feet while lying in my queen-sized bed. Ahhh, heaven.

It reminded me, of course, of that first night in North Carolina. The place where I planted the 20 fruit trees, mostly in the pouring rain. The place where I dug holes for my latrine 21 nights in a row, using them while coyotes howled. The place where I would probably not stay now, but am glad I did then because I simply could not quit right at the beginning after six solid months of planning. Plus, I ended up liking the host (a lot!), I learned a ton, and I feel like I made a difference. (Lish, in fact, sent me occasional updates on how things were growing, as did all my hosts, which I really enjoyed and appreciated).

That first night at Lish's farm in North Carolina, I thought I was going to die. It was maybe 30 degrees Fahrenheit/less than zero degrees Celsius, and my old, cluttered, dirty trailer had no heat. I thought again about that dusty propane heater Lish had given me to use, which was shooting up flames, so I envisioned either burning to death or freezing. I opted for the possibility of freezing and bundled myself up with everything I brought.

I smiled thinking about the next day there when that Amazon truck came rattling down the dirt and gravel road in the pitch black to deliver Smiley, and I stood right in the middle and waved my arms. Throughout the rest of my journey, there was only one happier moment, family experiences aside.

So here's to being cool when we're hot and warm when we're cold. Here's to bathrooms. Here's to not quitting. Here's to coming full circle and living to tell about it (or at least, that was looking hopeful).

Here's to Smiley.

My happiest moment, if you were wondering, happened in the old jail at the llama and lavender ranch. I cut armfuls of French lavender out in the field during what photographers call the "golden hour" late in the afternoon when the sun was just starting to dip. I then unlatched the jail door, squeezed my way into the comfortably-cool, unlit adobe room so that the kittens didn't get out, put on Parisian café music (taking a rare break from Momma's Adventure Playlist), and hung the rubber-banded lavender bunches with paper clips on nails on the wall to dry.

As the sun's striations cast a glow on the hanging bouquets and fallen buds on the concrete floor, my head became increasingly light from the soporific effect of the intoxicating fragrance. The kittens batted and climbed, and I honestly don't know if I will ever feel that happy again. Whatever you are imagining this scene to be like, it was even better. And then I got to do it again and again, day after day. There are, of course, TikToks.

I never thought I would fall in love again after Kansas — herding the alpacas out on the range, putting the chickens to bed, and riding my bike on those dirt roads. And then I did. In Spanish Fork, Utah, and in an old jail in California.

My husband and I had gone on a trip to four countries in Europe, before our older daughter was born, using travel points from my constant business trips with Turner Broadcasting. In Paris, I had bought a little bottle of lavender oil at an outdoor market and brought it back to my office at CNN Center in Downtown Atlanta, where I placed it on the edge of my desk on the eighth floor overlooking a parking deck. I opened it and smelled it every day at first, and then just occasionally (as these things go) and said to myself, "One day."

I had finally arrived at One Day.

Before I left Long Look Ranch, I scooped up a small handful of lavender buds from the floor of the jail and put them in a rubber band box. I then tucked it in my backpack to bring home to put by my bed to smell each day. I promised myself I would plant lavender in my garden. I did not want to stop living my lavender farm fantasy.

"Only 2,649.75 miles to go," I told Sarah, and we both laughed. We had just walked about a quarter mile/half a kilometer of the 2,650-mile/4,265 kilometer Pacific Crest Trail (the PCT) in Vasquez Rocks Natural Area and Nature Center, where episodes of *Star Trek* and movies such as *Planet of the Apes* and *The Flintstones* were filmed.

"We can tell folks for the rest of our lives that we are section-hiking," I added, as we posed in front of a PCT sign in downtown Agua Dulce that was dedicated to infamous trail angels Jeff and Donna Saufley. Trail angels provide free assistance such as food, water, accommodations or other support to hikers. Jeff and Donna opened their property to thousands of thru-hikers over the years, providing them with everything you can imagine.

Maybe Sarah and I would meet again someday on the PCT and add another quarter mile or so to our big accomplishment. Maybe she or I would be a trail angel some day. Maybe we already *were* trail angels to each other in our own special ways.

A couple of days later, a wildfire appeared over the ridge of a mountain near Long Look Ranch while we were painting a shed. Helicopters flew overhead. A quick online search revealed Los Angeles County and Angeles National Forest fire crews battled it successfully. Twenty-four acres/10 hectares right by where we had just been at Vasquez Rocks burned.

I asked Josette what our evacuation plan was, just as I had asked Sister Jane in Kansas where my safe spot was during a tornado. Josette told me we would load up the llamas in a truck and the community often worked together to evacuate animals. This was not a place unfamiliar with wildfires. In fact, it was the hot spot, so to speak, of multiple fires in the prior years. Smokey the Bear would be right at home here.

These llamas, as opposed to the ones in Utah who were halter, lead and pack-trained, were practically feral. I had seen how laborious it was when the ranch hands tried to move one male from the lower herd to the upper herd the prior week, and I could only imagine what loading them all up during a fire would be like. Considering my low position on the priority list here, I would clearly not survive a fire. This made me homesick for maybe the first real time. I missed folks who loved me and would make sure I didn't die in a fire.

While hopping a fence one day to feed the llamas, I realized that upper body strength, the fastest muscle mass to leave aging women, could mean the difference between life and death for me, along with squatting and swimming and bike riding. I may someday need to hop a fence to evacuate, or I may need to carry my belongings a long distance. I may also be in a position to carry a child or help hold up my mother, husband or a stranger in need. My ongoing fitness as long as possible was a survival tactic for both me and my community in case of fires or other climate impacts.

There had been a survival store on Main Street in Spanish Fork, Utah that included all the gadgets and gear you could possibly need to survive both everyday and Earth-shattering disasters. My physical fitness, however, was something I could maintain and improve myself that might make a life-saving difference — and it helped to have an action I could take, no matter how small.

Two llamas and a chicken did not survive my time at Long Look Ranch, by the way, and that had nothing to do with fires. That was just how things went on farms and ranches. I had seen five roosters die in North Carolina as well. Sensing their impending death, Lish and I had been hoping to bring them to a large cat (such as lions and tigers) sanctuary near Spinning Plates Farm as food, but they were too rotten by the time we got to them.

Sarah, Andrew and I buried the chicken and the ranch hands buried the llamas, which was difficult as the aquifer was so full from spring rains that it was hard to dig deep enough for burial without hitting water. Sarah and I placed flowers on all their graves and blessed the departure of their souls. *Hare Krishna.*

See all the fun things I got to experience and learn during this journey? Returning to the bottom of the hill in suburbia was going to be tricky.

My time nearing an end at Long Look Ranch, I was starting to envision that moment when I would finally reach the Pacific Ocean. *Peaceful* Ocean. How I would ride my bike down Venice Boulevard to the applause of my cheering family, the people who loved me and would save me in a fire. How we would walk down to the shoreline and I would dip my bike tire in the lapping waters, just as I did in the Atlantic Ocean's roar so many months ago.

When I got to this mobile home three weeks ago, I smiled when I saw a sign posted in the living room that said *Peace Love Chocolate*. It was a reminder of the Peaceful Ocean that was keeping me going (and a validation that I was smart to pick up a couple of bags of chocolate chips, as is my habit, before arriving).

And then my TikTok feed filled with the news of Maui and the recent hurricane. People jumped into that ocean to save their lives. People swam in the depth and darkness. People stood in the ash and embers. People drowned. Suddenly my vision of dipping my tire seemed small and stupid.

The Pacific Ocean saved — and stole — people's lives. How on Earth could I trivialize that by thinking what I was about to do was important? How could I show respect and yet celebrate my cross-country achievement, as is tradition for people on bikes? I thought of this often while riding my bike back and forth across these high-desert mountains. I didn't yet have the answers.

I did know, however, that struggles and traumas are not comparative. That, in fact, is where people are often surprised when someone who seems to have a good life *ends* their life — many people don't reach out for help because they don't feel, comparatively, that their situation is bad enough, or people tell them that they shouldn't feel a certain way because other people have it worse.

(Important: if you are considering causing harm to yourself, please call or text 988 in the United States. That is the Suicide Prevention Hotline. Trained professionals will communicate with you *with radical non-judgment* to connect you with resources or just to listen. As my sweatshirt says, and strangers tap me on the shoulder to thank me for it every single time I wear it in public, *the world is a better place with you in it. You are enough.*)

Joy will always be an act of resistance for me to the extraordinarily horrific things that are happening in this world — and an outward display of the insistence of the human spirit's ability to endure. Centering joy, even in darkness — especially in darkness — seems to be my calling, not just for my own self-preservation but as inspiration to others. Those increasingly indisputable facts had been reinforced for me over and over again throughout this journey.

I carry childhood trauma. I've experienced other struggles and lived realities — and, of course, there was that growing solastalgia, or climate grief. I was not at the place yet where I could see myself feeling joyful about the Pacific Ocean again, or even comfortable dipping that tire. I had a few more days yet to work it out with my Higher Power, and my bike.

I also wanted more chocolate.

And, yes, I could use more love.

The good news? Love (and chocolate) were coming. I was on my way back to Los Angeles in just a few days. Not only would I see my older daughter and her fiancé again (who were being given a bridal shower timed so I could attend), but my husband was currently driving cross-country to meet us, and my younger daughter would be flying in from New York City. I would somehow dip that bike tire. I would celebrate my cross-country achievement before the swoop through the Southwest back home. And I would turn 60, chocolate cake and all.

But first, the rattlesnake.

It was my final day at this llama ranch and lavender farm, and my final day of the entire journey being a WWOOFer. I raised a pitchfork over my head in glorious triumph. This was hard, and I had done it. *I did not quit.*

*Slow down, Cowgirl. Not so fast.*

Sarah, Josette, Sydney (this week's additional WWOOFer, who was currently out of a job due to the writers and actors strikes and who, like all the WWOOFers I met, was lovely), and I were at a picnic table nestled by the garden, bundling sage and English lavender we had just picked. We were going to bring it to another ranch's popular gift shop where some lavender products from the ranch (lavender salt and sugar) were already for sale.

I was excited to get off-ranch for only my second time since I got there, and for this specific micro-enterprise purpose. (I had also been involved when Sheila asked me to join her for the state inspection to become a certified Grown in California farm, which would mean she could then start selling at farmers markets. I really appreciated being included, and in fact, felt *necessary*, which meant a lot.)

And then one of the ranch hands walked over.

"Hey, I wanna show you something," he said. He held up a rattlesnake body, its tail still vibrating. He then tilted a large shovel he was carrying in his other hand so we could see clearly. On it was a head. The head of the snake. Mouth open. Still trying to attack.

"It was in the French lavender field," he stated, matter-of-factly.

The field where I cut armfuls of lavender every day. Where I danced to Parisian café music. Where I lived my best lavender farm fantasy.

Where I clearly could have died.

I knew I would never set foot in that field again.

The next day, I was, thankfully, on the road again. I had somehow survived my most extreme landscape of the past five months. Goodbye, mountain lions, coyotes, scorpions, rattlesnakes and wildfires.

I didn't yet know about the historic hurriquake-to-come and the 2:00 AM rideshare that would go horribly wrong. Two different cities. Two different stories. Too close to home — and my 60th birthday — to end this journey tragically.

# 9

## Sweet Endings

**W**heat, I said to myself over and over again, *lots of wheat; a tremendous amount of wheat,* replacing my *trust the journey* mantra with lines from the classic movie *Love and Death,* said by the Woody Allen character the day before he was scheduled to be executed. I thought the comedic image of Woody Allen combined with a calming memory of Kansas might help. No. My full-blown panic was just seconds away, and I wanted love, not death.

I was in a car, and this is never a good place for me. I wasn't nervous because of my older daughter's driving (although cars, in general made me anxious, as you know). I was nervous about the hurricane moving in on Los Angeles and our journey on the 405 to her bridal shower, where visibility was approaching close to zero and numerous motor vehicles were already hydroplaning. I was with both my daughters, and the possibility of losing all of us was just too much to bear. Plus, I had woken up with a throbbing ear ache that was getting worse by the minute.

Scheduled for a restaurant in Topanga Canyon, the shower had been changed last-minute to her fiancé's family's home in the Valley because the canyon was already flooded. The weather was expected to get much worse that day and all the guests were told to prepare to stay overnight, if needed. A brunch for the guys was already canceled.

I had seen the media coverage of Los Angeles in torrential storms, how the infrastructure was not built for that amount of water and the flooding can be deadly. My heart raced. My ear pounded. *Breathe, breathe, breathe,* I reminded myself over and over while gripping the door handle like a security blanket. And to think I had come to Los Angeles to relax after my constantly-stressful journey!

*And then the earthquake happened.* We were at the shower, all scattered around the living room, kitchen and dining room. I was sitting on a couch, my body never quite back to neutral since the car ride. When the whole house started shaking, I just closed my eyes and took a deep breathe. You think you get 80 years; I wasn't going to get 60.

The day before, with news of the storm on its way, I had decided to dip my bike tire in the Pacific Ocean right away just in case I didn't get another chance to do so due to flooding or whatever else fate might bring. I had made peace with this decision. My family met me at the Venice Pier — I rode my bike there, singing songs from Momma's Adventure Playlist at the top of my lungs, tears streaming down my face. I had done it. *We* had done it.

My husband got in position to film from the pier while my daughters and future son-in-law walked with me down to the ocean. As we were about to step off the pier onto the sand, there was a little girl with a bicycle. She and I locked eyes, as always happens when I pass girls with my bikes, and my older daughter saw me swallow hard. She knew why, but I don't know if she knew the extent of it.

This happened all the time with me and little girls, and had been happening for years. In fact, the week of my 55th birthday, exactly five years ago to the week, I wrote this blog post:

*Every time I pass a little girl on a bike, she stares at me. Not just looks. Stares. Every single time. It is not uncommon for a girl I pass to literally just stop completely and stare at me right in the middle of the path. This doesn't happen with boys, and this doesn't happen with older girls or women. Men will often (but not always) do the "bike nod" hello, but only if I'm on my road bike (rarely if I'm on an upright bike). But little girls — they are watching, and they are learning from us, my fellow women-on-bikes. They are taking it all in, how expansive a definition it is to be female, to be a woman, to age. As I celebrate my 50th year as a bike rider this week (having learned to ride when I was five), I am reminded of the little girl inside of me, who is still watching . . . and learning.*

I wrote the following poem about an experience I had with a girl on the sidelines of a bike class I taught, which I wrote about in my book *Traveling at the Speed of Bike*. Maybe, at the end of the day, the poem was really about myself. Perhaps you see yourself in it as well.

> *Dear Girl*
> *I just want you to know I saw the magnitude of your strength*
> *And how you allowed yourself to hope*
> *Against your better judgment*
> *That perhaps this time would be different,*
> *That the bigness in you would be perceived,*
> *Believed*
> *And you could be more fully, expansively,*
> *In all your unbridled glory*
> *Your fiercest*
> *Dearest girl;*
> *I just want you to know*
> *I saw.*

There's another story about a girl in a pink jacket in that book. I had taken my road bike down from the attic and gotten it fixed up after 20 years of neglect while I hauled lunches and violins back and forth to my daughters' schools with them on my cheap upright bike from Target. My first time back on my beloved road bike (which my husband had bought me as a wedding gift), I encountered a flood. I watched as a girl in a pink jacket rode her bike right through it, but I was too scared to do so. I have thought of that girl in the pink jacket every single day of my life since then.

I have *become* the girl in the pink jacket. I have ridden through my own personal floods.

Stranded by buses. Scalded by heat. And yes, even stalked by a rattlesnake. Plus, there was an eye infection in Kansas and this ear infection in Los Angeles, and more splinters, scratches, cuts and bites than I could count (shout-out to Sister Imelda for her itchy scratchy balm). Yes, I was grateful to have survived many physical challenges while traveling *Round America with a Duck*.

The mental challenges were even harder. Feeling vulnerable. Scared. Sometimes lonely. Helpless. Hopeless. Occasionally mistreated. Once even completely forgotten.

My family held me up throughout the journey and then, in real life, right there on the ocean's edge after I ceremoniously and exuberantly dipped that damn tire, as I did at the Atlantic Ocean months ago, signifying I had made it coast to coast. It was one of the best moments of my life.

And now, as I sat there in the middle of a hurriquake with my very own two little girls, now women, I knew for real, for sure, *forever*, that the only way forward was not only to trust the journey. But to trust *myself*.

I made good decisions. About marriage. About children. About work. About life. About this journey. I could "make do" when required and pivot when needed. And I could dance every step of the way.

I felt so strong and solid in these realizations, sitting there on that couch as the house once again became steady and the rains lightened temporarily, that what happened next shocked me. In fact, it was the only regret of my entire journey.

*I canceled my birthday party.*

My husband had planned a lovely dinner at a nice restaurant with our daughters and future in-laws for the night after the bridal shower, two days before my actual birthday because our younger daughter was flying back to New York City.

We had met his family in person for the first time the day before the bridal shower at a very enjoyable outdoor lunch in downtown Culver City right after the tire dip, where the group conversation flowed naturally and I also got to know her future father-in-law one-on-one a bit as we sat next to each other. We were all shoulder-to-shoulder, and I felt fresh and clean, thanks to my older daughter.

I had ridden my bike a total of 26 miles/42 kilometers that morning (my longest ride in weeks after being so isolated in the High Desert) and ended up at my daughter's apartment bursting with endorphins and not that much time to spare before the scheduled lunch. She insisted I shower the sand and sweat off me.

"I'll just freshen up," I said.

She handed me a towel and said as diplomatically as she could considering there was no time to waste, "You stink. You have never met them before. Please shower."

So, I did. First impressions matter. We don't stand on ceremony in our family, but a basic level of hygiene is a fair expectation. It was the second impression that I ended up screwing up.

Before we left the bridal shower the next day, the hurricane was downgraded to a tropical storm but was still expected to rage into the night. I said it was just too much to bear, not knowing how the day was going to shake out and what the impact of the storm was going to be on the city. I told everyone it was best to cancel the dinner party. My husband asked emphatically if I was sure, I said yes, and he canceled the reservation.

I am fully aware that I simply panicked, or maybe I was still panicking from the car. Either way, I made a mistake. I shouldn't have made that decision. It could have at least waited until the next morning. I don't need to ask you this time — I was, indeed, the asshole.

I apologized afterwards. I acknowledged that I was struggling a bit being with a crowd of people — maybe I always did, in fact. It was especially hard for me to go from practically feral myself, like the High Desert llamas, these past five months to operating within society again. I was always on the edge of that anyway, so I think it was just too much for me all at once.

*You are enough,* I reminded myself, thinking back to my sweatshirt. But I realized re-entry back to my prior life might not be so easy. Maybe I had changed too much to fit in anymore, not that I ever did. Maybe I never wanted to try to fit in again.

That next day, the sun shone brightly, the storm having passed without too much damage. Our family pivot included a casual birthday dinner at my daughter and fiancé's apartment instead. My husband took me out to a farm-to-table restaurant in Venice for brunch on my actual birthday.

On my way there, a Happy Birthday balloon blew across the multi-use path on the beach where I was riding, if you can believe it. I tied it to my handlebars and strangers wished me happy birthday that entire day. I also passed both a sculpture and a mural of a camel, further solidifying my unintentional camelid tour of America.

As day fell into evening, we had dinner at a beach shack by the ocean (per my request) as we watched the sunset, just the two of us, my husband and me, our paper plates in our laps, our feet in the sand. Everything about that simple dinner was absolutely perfect.

Later that week, I taught my daughter's future sister-in-law how to ride a bike on a path on a cliff in Santa Monica overlooking the Pacific Ocean. I then took a lovely walk there with my daughter's future mother-in-law, ending with yet another dance up a set of steps. That would be four staircases during this journey — the Rocky steps, the Salt Lake City rainbow steps, the Krishna temple steps, and now the Santa Monica steps. So maybe it all worked out for the best.

I rode my bike, danced, and made TikToks all over the Los Angeles area, including at the sign on the Santa Monica Pier indicating the end of Route 66. I was a long way from the Route 66 sign in Joplin, where I danced in the rain after visiting the memorial sculptures, mosaic and butterfly garden of the country's most deadly tornado, which killed 161 people, and viewed the butterfly murals all around the city commemorating the "butterfly people," whom children who survived the tornado said protected them. We all need butterfly people to protect us from climate change, it seems.

Riding an average of 20 miles/32 kilometers a day the 10 days I was there, I realized Los Angeles could be one of the great bike cities in the world. A lot of the city is flat and built on a grid, the weather is mostly great (hurriquake and wildfires aside), and the culture is relatively supportive (I didn't have one close-pass or harassment incident the whole time I was there).

Almost every bike I saw on the UCLA and USC campuses was colorful and had a vintage design, which was fun and inviting (and you know how the girlies love the vibes, according to that TikTok sound). Some of the existing bike infrastructure is already world-class but there is lots of room for improvement — just like everywhere in the USA, it seems.

After my husband left to drive back home, I stayed a few extra days with my older daughter and her fiancé, just as I had before the final llamas and lavender. It was so nice to be a part of their everyday lives. To meet their friends. Visit that book store again. Run errands. Hang out. Pick up Thai food, which dangled off my handlebars as I rode the wonderful protected bike lane on Venice Boulevard. I even got to help my daughter repot her plants, which we identified with Caru's app.

I also passed not one but two more rainbows — a mural on Melrose Avenue (where I danced, of course), and a 94-foot-high rainbow sculpture at Sony Pictures Studios (where picketers marched) that serves as a tribute to, yes, *The Wizard of Oz*.

I thought of my friend, Brad, who gave me both the sun hat and the duck hat. He dreams of becoming a full-time screenwriter and has been writing, networking, entering (and winning) contests and getting so close to his pot at the end of the rainbow so many times. When we worked together at Turner Broadcasting in the 1990s, he started wearing a watch with two faces— one with East Coast time and one with Hollywood time, as he put it. His time is coming.

My time here was ending. I had a few more things to find in LA before leaving. My final day in that City of Angels, one of the rare days I didn't high-tail it to the beach as part of my bike route (where I wrote more bad poetry on a rock jetty as an homage to my teenage self), I did a big loop on my bike around Beverly Hills, even getting a photo of my ducks Disco and Robin by an iconic Beverly Hills sign.

After then passing through West Hollywood and heading towards Pico Robertson, I suddenly smelled a very strong and pungent odor. It was tar, undeniably tar, but unlike anything I had ever smelled before. Not a road being paved. Something more *prehistoric*.

Sure enough, as I rounded the corner from West 6th Street to South Curson Avenue, I fell upon the La Brea Tar Pits. *What fresh hell was this?* I wondered. I walked my bike down to an oozing, bubbling pit of pith, fake wooly mammoths standing in the middle of it.

This still-active paleontological research site exudes thousands of years of natural asphalt (called brea in Spanish), the methane that's released causing the constant bubbling. Bones of trapped animals have been preserved there for centuries, including saber-tooth cats, horses, coyotes and large bison (bison!). Only one human's remains have every been found there. A woman.

I stood there watching the bubbles and thinking about that woman being stuck, thinking about any woman anywhere being stuck in their circumstances, in the humdrums, in the muck of it all in this thing called life.

I thought of myself and how liberating this journey had been. How I never wanted to be stuck again. And then I wondered *how do I go back while still moving forward at the same time? Was that even possible?*

Three days on trains were about to give me time to think about that, or maybe not even think at all. To *just be*.

We were three hours behind and no one seemed to mind as the train wound its way through deserts, skirted the Mexican border and swooped upward toward the Bayou.

Catcaw acacia and camel (camelid!) grass gave way to Southern live oak and Eastern pine. I could almost start to smell the proverbial barn of home, although I still had 36 hours and a night in New Orleans to go before I crossed that familiar threshold.

We were suspended in time here together, a Babel Tower of accents and skin tones, the sun rising and setting around us. Some of us changed clothes from day to day. Some didn't. I wore new llama t-shirts my family gave me for my birthday last week (as an homage to the three herds of llamas and herd of alpacas with which I worked during this journey).

The viewing car on the train had become our community center. There was frequent laughter. People watched each other's things while they went to the bathroom. I tipped folks off to where the unused wet bar was with the free potable tap water so they didn't have to keep buying bottled water. We said good morning, good night, sleep well.

It was nice — and nice, frankly, is underrated.

I started to sort through five months of photos and videos from this journey. I read a book. I scribbled in my journal. I texted my family. I listened as people told me their life stories — one guy saved a man from drowning! Learn to swim, folks (and brush your hair).

I stared out the window while watching the landscape shift. I started to drift, that scarf from Janet wrapped around my head, night falling, me slipping in and out of sleep. *Chug, chug, chug, chug.* The train inched along. We seemed suspended in time in our shared liminal space.

By the end of the second day, my oranges all shared, I was starting to look ahead. This train ended in New Orleans and I had reserved a hostel in the French Quarter overnight, although it would be early morning by the time we arrived due to our delay. The train to Atlanta wouldn't leave until 9:00 AM and that would get in at 11:00 PM, if all went well.

My husband would meet me at the station, just as he had dropped me off at the transit station to meet that first bus by the curb. We were still together, and, in fact, better than ever. There had been no way of knowing how this would have gone. I could be on the back of a motorcycle right now, or still on my high horse in the High Desert.

I would then have a day or two to settle in, and then it would be Pie Weekend. That was Labor Day Weekend, which was the time right after the start of school when all the club sign-ups and commitments used to be due, when my daughters were younger and it always overwhelmed me. We started this annual tradition of buying and eating our very own pies, however we wanted, while making pie charts about how we wished to spend the precious, nonrenewable gift of 168 hours that make up a week. This always helped us figure out our priorities at a time we (or, at least I, as a young working mother) felt pulled in many directions.

It was always amazing to see what suddenly dropped off our lists, and helpful to learn what each other's priorities were. My younger daughter, for instance, always designated a big section on her pie chart just for thinking, so I was always careful to leave her alone when she needed more time to just sit. I designate a big part of my time to thinking now, too. Wise child.

Although my daughters are grown and gone now into their next phases of life, I still do Pie Weekend. So I was already salivating about the chocolate cream pie I would buy when I got home, visualizing how I would eat it all weekend long, whipped cream first, on that old couch we all love so much in which I haven't sunk my body, now a new age, since March.

I would catch up with my husband. I would see my mother. I would trim the bushes. I would ask anyone and everyone those four magic words: "Can I help you?"

But not yet.

These final hours of this unforgettable, unrepeatable time in my life were just for me. They were for gazing out the window. For breathing in, breathing out. For just being. And I was going to drink them up, freely, like water from the tap.

That was, of course, if I survived New Orleans. And that became questionable very quickly.

"I'm starting to get very worried," my husband texted.

I had texted him at 2:59 AM Central Time and told him my train had just arrived in New Orleans, four hours late.

I had a reservation at a hostel less than a mile away and decided to still go there despite the late hour with the hopes of getting maybe two hours sleep and a shower after the past two days and nights on the train from Los Angeles. It was keyless entry at the hostel, however, and I was nervous, but I also did not want to spend the night at the train station, as some of my train mates (most notably my new friend Joshua, who had been sitting behind me and with whom I enjoyed pleasant conversations) were doing.

Grateful to not have spent a fortune at a "real" hotel (but still a hundred bucks), I ordered a rideshare and went outside to wait for it, after checking that it seemed safe to do so. My husband, who was still awake on Eastern Time, planned to follow my travels on his phone.

The driver arrived and it was a woman, which, like in Boulder, gave me some relief. I was safe. Or so I thought.

I loaded up her trunk and she started driving. And driving. And *driving*. I asked her, "Where are you going?"

She said, "These are the directions to the address."

I could see on her dashboard that she had entered the correct address. I had mapped it already, however (originally hoping to just ride my bike there if we had arrived on time) and knew it was less than a mile/a little over a kilometer from the station. Minutes. And we were already way beyond that.

"This is much farther than I expected," I said, thinking maybe there was construction. Maybe there was an explanation that made sense. "How much farther are you going?"

She said several more miles. I looked out my window and we had left the French Quarter a long time ago. We were in a grittier part of town, possibly heading toward my abduction?

I contemplated what I should do. I couldn't just jump out of the car, for two good reasons: (1) I'd be stranded in an isolated, edgy area, and (2) all my stuff, including my getaway bicycle, was in the trunk.

"Please pull over," I finally said firmly. "This is wrong."

If she didn't pull over, I knew I would need to make a more drastic decision. For one thing, I had pre-entered 911 on my phone.

She pulled over. I showed her my map. She told me that the rideshare's GPS sometimes completely screwed up, so she entered the address on her personal phone and then followed the new route. We were back on track.

I hadn't seen my husband's text because I was hyper-focused on what was happening. He then added another one.

"Please text as soon as you can. You are so far away from the hotel. Damn. It was only a mile away."

"We are lost," I replied. "It's a woman and I am safe. We are turning back."

"I was about 30 seconds away from calling the police," he added.

I was still on high alert, however, as my driver pulled down the alley where my hostel was and stopped in front of the address. There was a man lingering outside the door. I asked her if she would stay until I got in, knowing I now needed to use a keyless entry code while juggling all my stuff, making me extra vulnerable.

She got out of the car with me and helped me with my stuff. The guy said a nice hello. Maybe he was a guest at the hostel, too. He seemed to just be having a cigarette break, or, as the train conductors like to call them, a *fresh air break*. He wasn't waiting to kill me.

Safely ensconced in the lobby (with yet two more keyless entry codes before I would finally get to my room), I texted my husband that I had arrived. He replied that he was already ready to book me at the nice hotel down the block in case I had any problems getting in.

I took the elevator up a flight, after waving a quick hello to two people on their computers in the lobby. I dropped my stuff in my tiny, perfect room, the bunk bed fitting wall to wall and me having no need for anything else besides a shower. Someone came into the lovely non-gendered bathroom down the hall, which had multiple private rooms inside it with toilets and showers, while I was leaving after taking truly one of the best hot showers of the entire journey.

Back in my private room, I climbed into the bottom bunk, set my alarm for two hours away, wrapped my head with Janet's bike scarf, and fell fast asleep.

Just before the crack of dawn, I woke up, packed up, danced, and hula-hooped in the third and final place during this journey (the hayloft at the alpaca ranch in Kansas, in the driveway at Elise's home with Laure in Boulder, and here in a hostel in the French Quarter in New Orleans, where I found the hula hoop by the foosball table). Then I and the ducks and Willie Nelson got on the road again for the very last time.

The sun rose as I rode my bike along the Mississippi River, passing a paddlewheel boat and a fence with love locks, those personalized padlocks that serve as symbols of commitments between couples locked onto bridges around the world.

I had one destination and one destination only: Cafe du Monde. Come hell or high water or fire or rattlesnakes, I was going to get those beignets. I had, in fact, promised I'd bring some back for my new friend Joshua, who I'd see again at the station for our final train to Atlanta.

No longer open 24 hours, as was its tradition, Cafe du Monde opened at 7:00 AM, and I was first in line. The clerk, named Grayland, greeted me warmly. I bought extra servings of beignets to share with Joshua and my other train-mates back at the station, and to bring some home. They dangled off my handlebars as I ate puffy dough piping hot, bite by bite, while riding my bike through the French Quarter, powdered sugar dotting my cheeks, shirt and bike and flying off me into the already stifling, humid air.

People waved and raised their cups of coffee to my beignets as I passed. I blew into New Orleans Union Station (not to be confused with the Denver Union Station or Los Angeles Union Station), and raised my bags of beignets triumphantly to my fellow train passengers, who clapped and circled around to enjoy them. I may not have ever had a more glorious start to a day, and I've had lots of them I've loved, especially during this five-month, 10,000-mile/16,100-kilometer journey *Round America with a Duck*.

Fourteen hours after my train crossed Lake Pontchartrain during the anniversary of Hurricane Katrina on the longest overwater train bridge in the world, we slipped below Peachtree Street to my final destination. Atlanta, Georgia. *Home.*

I felt like Dorothy waking up in Kansas again (ahhh, Kansas!). Like Dorothy, would I decide to never leave my home again? Or did Dorothy, in fact, start planning her next adventure the very next day? Have we heard Dorothy's complete story, the what-happens-next? A quick search revealed that *The Wizard of Oz* was actually a long-running book series and Dorothy returned to Oz many times.

I sang *we may never pass this way again* throughout my journey, reminding myself to savor each moment. But would I return? And if so, where? Do I go back to Kansas and possibly alter or even ruin the memory (or, of course, make even better additional memories), or do I just cherish what I already experienced and move on? What about the Krishna temple and Spanish Fork, Utah? The llama and lavender farm in the High Desert of California? The book club in Chapel Hill?

My husband and I now knew (or, rather, confirmed yet again) that our nontraditional approach to fulfilling our own personal callings while staying together worked. And I knew that there are WWOOF farms everywhere. I valued my excellent reviews, Candida aside, because I was hoping to travel the world, maybe for just a month a year, and the positive reviews would help me land future positions. First up, perhaps, would be Ireland, from where my mother's parents emigrated to the United States a hundred years ago.

With all the unrest both climate-wise and politically in the United States, I was considering applying for dual citizenship there, which would extend that citizenship opportunity for two more generations and enable my progeny to travel freely, live and work in many countries. It would keep options open, and right now, options seem important.

I would need to submit a ton of very valuable original documents about my grandparents and was thinking about delivering them in

Dublin in person. Right off the coast of Dublin, there's apparently a WWOOF location with sheep and wallabies. *Wallabies!*

My mind tossed that over and over again until it wandered on to the next topic. There was never enough time on the buses and trains for thinking about all these things. I never tired of it. I never got bored. People would say to me afterwards when I told them about my journey, their fixation on bathrooms, food and fear, "I could never do that."

My friend Donna — the one who said yes when a motorcyclist crossed *her* path, married him, and was volunteering with him as docents on a conservation island off the coast of Florida when I spoke with her — told me that when people say that to her (which they do often), she replies, "You probably couldn't."

I understood what she meant now. My journey *Round America with a Duck* was hard. It took a certain kind of person and a certain kind of attitude, plus a willingness to change. To pivot. To trust the journey. Believing *I can do this* was the bare minimum for achieving it, and anyone who says they can't, really, truly can't. If you're thinking, *well, maybe I can*, then it's for you. It's that *maybe* where the magic lives.

That's where pilot-testing helped me. My two-week stay in the tiny home at a local nonprofit farm, my visit to a local Krishna temple, and my bus day-trip to a nearby city in the pouring rain all helped me see that yes, I could do this. And now I did. Now, *we* did. Me, my husband, my family, my friends, my WWOOF hosts, people I met along the way who shared their hope with me, and folks on TikTok. Maybe even you. Maybe there's been a ripple effect that I don't see yet. Maybe together we can cause our own positive storm this time.

I was emotional as I left the final train for the final time, filled with excitement and ennui in equal measure. My eyes moist, I trudged (for the last time) up the long staircase to a waiting room full of people going elsewhere. Washington. Philly. New York. Starting their own journeys. Leaving, to one day arrive somewhere new.

My sweet husband greeted me, both of us so relieved I had survived this crazy escapade. Truth? I was scared every single day. It shouldn't be so scary to travel around our own country, but it is. And with our escalating climate crisis, I, unfortunately, expect that will only get worse, which is one of the reasons I rushed to publish this book.

Maybe something you read about my experience will inspire you to make one small change or advocate for increased resiliency where you live. That may be the simple and joyful act of replacing one motor vehicle trip with a bike ride. If you are a woman and don't think that matters, note that women make or influence something like 80% of all consumer purchase decisions, we are more likely to make eco-friendly decisions when it is safe and convenient to do so, we frequently do something called "trip-chain" (which means make multiple stops), and we shop locally more when on bikes (as do all people on bikes), which keeps more money circulating in our local economies. Plus, little girls (and boys) are watching us.

So, yes. One little bike ride does makes a difference. *The world is a better place with you in it,* as my sweatshirt says, but I can't help adding to that *especially when you ride a bike.*

My bike, which I finally named America, cost $350. It folded up. It fit everywhere. It was fun. It started conversations, especially about its paint job and the ducks on its handlebars. And it rode beautifully throughout this entire journey, with a little help from a couple of bike shops along the way. You don't need anything fancy to help our world's future. *You are enough* on the bike that may be in your garage or basement or attic right now or the new one that you can afford on your budget. If hills or heat are holding you back, consider an e-bike.

Before we left the station, by the way, my husband took the final video of the trip, just as he had taken the first one on that rainy, cold morning back in March when he dropped me off for that bus heading to the repurposed tobacco farm in North Carolina.

We arrived home just after midnight (cue the song "Midnight Train to Georgia"), and it was all so surreal to me. The house felt huge (and spotlessly clean), the gardens lush (and lovingly tended), my little bag of everything I've needed eclipsed by all this other stuff I one day thought I needed, too.

I reminded myself that I had cleaned so much out (as had my husband while I was gone), and yes, perhaps this carefully-curated selection from my life was just right for here, for now. My other bikes. My roller skates. The garden tools. My laptop (oh, how I'd missed that, laboriously tapping out my blog posts on my phone throughout the journey).

I had to allow myself some time to adjust, but the questions that had been gathering in my head loomed. How do I come back while still moving forward? How do we craft a future that's fulfilling in a world in flux? Where do we go from here, figuratively, literally? All questions that were too big for that morning.

I enjoyed my shower without having to turn on a well and watch for scorpions. My freezer and cupboard were full, and I had clothing choices beyond the five or six things I'd been wearing. My husband even bought me the chocolate cream pie I wanted for my upcoming Pie Weekend.

When I woke up the next morning, a stack of *Ducks Unlimited* magazines waiting for me (I had joined this conservation organization dedicated to preserving wetlands for wild fowl prior to departure), I warmed up a Cafe du Monde beignet and ate it, powdered sugar falling all over my face and llama shirt in the humid air.

As I thought about planting in my garden, I also started pondering the idea of going back to the community garden, lock and all, to ask those four magic words I learned to respect in North Carolina and throughout this journey: *Can I help you?* Maybe it was time I came off my high horse.

And in that moment celebrating such a sweet ending to a life-changing experience, I realized, without a doubt, that there was, indeed, a way forward.

But I still had one more thing to do.

# 10

## Making a Mark

The needle ripped through my skin, signaling not pain but presence. It was my first tattoo, and I felt it in a way I hadn't felt anything else in life. This seemed, suddenly, the perfect conclusion to a journey that flooded me with feelings, with presence, every single day.

I chose to replicate my words and handwriting from the beach when I dipped my bike tire in the Atlantic Ocean, when I was still so unsure I could achieve what I set out to do. My daughters later wrote those words, *Trust the Journey*, on the Pacific Ocean beach as well, when I dipped my other tire months later.

They are the words I say at the end of many of my TikToks. They are the words on the cover of my book, *Traveling at the Speed of Bike*. They are my mantra, my *Hare Krishna Hare Krishna Rama Rama Hare Hare*. They keep me going. And now, I finally fully and whole-heartedly believed them.

Throughout my journey, I wore that sweatshirt (tied around my waist when it got too hot) that held a message for the people behind me when I traveled on buses and trains and through cities and supermarkets. Almost every time I wore it, someone came up to me and thanked me, often with tears in their eyes. People are hurting everywhere, you know, perhaps you or someone you love as well. Small messages help.

And so, I had my three little encouraging words positioned on my body so that they could be viewed from the back of me. From people on line. From people passing. Standing. Ruminating. Thinking. Feeling big, painful thoughts and wondering if and how they could go on.

Maybe by moving my body in time, space and motion, I can help. Maybe even by doing nothing, by just being, *I am enough.* Making a mark in life is important, and maybe this small reminder to others — and myself — is a mark I can make.

Thank you for joining me on this journey. If you've been waiting for a sign to do your own journey, this is your sign. If you're scared, try pilot-testing it first; then, do it scared. If you have a different idea, but keep putting it off because the timing is not right, stop waiting. *We may never pass this way again.*

Someone identified as J.A. shared this quote in the Hermitage cabin's visitor log book in Kansas:

*When we walk to the end of all the light we have*
*And take the steps into darkness of the unknown*

*We must believe one of two things will happen . . .*
*There will be something solid for us to stand on,*
*Or we will be taught to fly.* —P. Overton

I know, in my heart of hearts, I did this journey on a wing and a prayer — my silly duck who helped me, anal-Virgo at heart, learn to "wing it"; and my higher power who kept putting signs of hope in my path, mostly through people. And through it all there was a *wind* beneath my wings, and for that, I thank my husband. I could not have done this without him.

I'm not the only one who did something different. Since I got home, I heard Bernard in New York City got his bike painted; Terra and James in Kansas bought their own farm; and Elise in Boulder started selling her crops to a restaurant again.

What is it *you* want to do?

All things are difficult until they are easy.

Don't quit before the miracle.

Your Kansas is coming.

*Trust the journey.*

## ACKNOWLEDGMENTS

It's humbling — and hard — to do work that challenges me physically and mentally as an experiential writer, and live to tell the story. I could not do it alone. Thank you to the WWOOF USA organization, and especially to my WWOOF hosts for opening up your lives to me and for your generous reviews. They will help me to continue my work close to home and around our shared world. Big thanks also to my family, friends, fellow WWOOFers, and the fine folks working with bikes, buses, and trains across the USA. As my sweatshirt says, the world is a better place with you in it. A special shout-out to my creative team — you helped me bring this book to life in record time, and I greatly appreciate you. We are better together. Oh, and a little kiss on the head to Disco and his side-duck, Robin. Thanks for shaking your tail feathers with me. That was a *ride*. Where to next?

## REVIEWS FROM WWOOF HOSTS

### Alicia/Lish (Spinning Plates Farm, North Carolina)
### United States • April 2023

Pattie is a miracle worker. She started up our farm this spring, despite heavy rains, almost single-handedly. She worked tirelessly and often independently to ensure our large kitchen garden and two dozen fruit trees got planted, the chickens got fed and eggs gathered, and the goats got cuddled and cared for. She was interested in helping with everything from dump runs to tractor driving. She even took bike rides with our dog! She is practical and reasonable and gives good advice. Her positive energy, especially with my children, was deeply appreciated and will be sorely missed.

### Christi (Heartland Farm, Kansas)
### United States • May 2023

Pattie was supposed to come for two weeks, and the stars aligned just right, and we got her for five weeks. What a blessing to the farm Pattie was. She was very quick to learn the routine and was not afraid of hard work. She did whatever was asked of her and did it with enthusiasm and a smile on her face. When we had other volunteers here, she would take them under her wing and show them what to do and work alongside them in harmony. Pattie got along with everyone, and everyone got along with Pattie. She brought her bike with her and would go explore the countryside on her bike along with Disco Duck and Disco Duck's buddy. Besides Pattie's outstanding work ethics, she is a brilliant social media content creator. She even helped the staff with a few social media issues, and they very much appreciated all the help. I could go on and on about how wonderful Pattie is, but you really need to experience the brilliance of Pattie at your place. The day she left we had a going-away party and I know tears were shed, especially me, as she was such an inspiration to me. Pattie will always be welcomed back with open arms and an open door. I am glad she trusted her journey and reached out to us.

## Elise (Pleasant Ridge Organics, Colorado) United States • June 2023

Pattie was at my homestead (not a working commercial farm) for three weeks. She brought tremendous joy and enthusiasm to the chores and people she encountered. Her stamina and strength were remarkable and she loved a shovel and pitchfork to my delight. Diligently, she achieved a lot each day and the improvements are noticeable. She was comfortable with cooking her own meals, sharing her favorite recipes and joining in with group meals.

She is a strict yet creative vegetarian. She was conversational and well versed in sustainability and all in the household enjoyed the interactions. Her passion for all things bicycle propelled her to visit and run errands near and far with her bicycle, often to my amazement as the weather was a challenge. Pattie arrives without a car so she would not be able to do chores with her own vehicle if that is needed, but the bicycle didn't hold her back from getting anywhere, really. Pattie has a vibrancy and passion for everything she gets involved with and I think she would be an asset to places that she intends to visit on her remarkable journey documenting women traveling by bicycle.

## Caru (Krishna Community, Utah) United States • July 2023

Pattie was a super volunteer. She worked hard in the garden at a time when tons of zucchinis and cucumbers were coming in. She picked a wheelbarrow of both almost daily and kept the plants from being attacked by squash bugs, which were bad in 2023. She didn't have a car but would go off on long adventurous bike rides and write her articles. Every exchange with her was positive, happy and upbeat. She is very hard working, smart and extremely self reliant. Any WWOOF host would be lucky to have her on site. Five stars totally!

## Sheila (Long Look Ranch, California)
## United States • August 2023

Pattie was a superb volunteer to have on our ranch. She had such a positive attitude and was always eager to try new things. A self starter and team player, she volunteered tirelessly in our lavender fields and helped us with this year's harvest. Regardless of the activity, she joined in whole heartedly whether it was weeding or ensuring all the livestock had plenty of water for the hot days. She set a tremendous example. Her enthusiasm was contagious and inspired other volunteers. Always interested in expanding her knowledge, she participated in our inspection for certification as a producer for farmer's markets and contributed valuable ideas. We would love to have Pattie join us on our ranch again anytime. Any farm or ranch would be lucky to have Pattie join their team!

If you enjoyed this book, please consider leaving a positive review on popular book sites. I'm an indie author and your support is greatly appreciated. Thanks.

Visit RoundAmericaWithADuck.com